Yes Changes Everything!

Yes Changes Everything!

*Free your inner awesome...
one yes at a time!*

Diana Davin
Blossie's Books
www.blossiesbooks.com

© 2020 Diana Davin. All rights reserved. No part of this book may be reproduced or transmitted in any form or by any means, electronic or mechanical, including photocopying, recording, or by any information storage and retrieval system, without permission in writing from the publisher.

Published by Blossie's Books
1-201-450-3654
E-mail: info@blossiesbooks.com
www.blossiesbooks.com
ISBN 13: 978-1-891019-45-6

Also by Diana Davin

Available in print and ebook format on amazon and barnesandnoble.com

Make this book your own
Everyone comes to a book like this at different points. Make this book your own by looking for the ideas that make the most sense for you. Then, go be awesome by using these ideas when, how, and where they fit your unique and beautiful life.

Disclaimer
Blossie's Books aim to help you open your mind and eyes to an amazing, high potential future and build the life you want. Your results, however, are your responsibility. Blossiesbooks.com does not provide legal, health, or financial advice and does not guarantee the results obtained by readers of its books, blogs, website, or any other materials.

Privacy
As always, the names I use in my stories have been changed to protect the privacy of my friends and clients.

Welcome to Blossie's Books!

Blossie's Books are for you, beautiful someone, as you wake up to the wildly awesome person you are.

Every Blossie's Book is a quick read of simple ideas for how to live life happy, healthy, sane and more awesome than ever. Read one with your coffee or lunch and start using the ideas right away.

The Gift of No, *Dream Come True*, and *You Know What I ~~Should Have~~ Said?* were just the beginning. There's much more…and still more to come!

Write to me at diana@blossiesbooks.com. I so want to hear your awesome story!

And thank you, THANK YOU for buying one of Blossie's Books!

Now go be awesome!

Contents

The Story of *Yes Changes Everything!* — 1
So why <u>not</u> yes? — 11

— PART 1 —

There's yes...then there's the yes that changes everything — 17
The yes that changes everything fits our plans and values — 27
The yes that changes everything has a positive purpose — 31
The yes that changes everything is right — right now — 37
Making room for *yes*! — 41
We are already brave — 65

— PART 2 —

"Only good things" — 75
    Yes builds our confidence — 77
    Yes is a fountain of youth — 89
    Yes brings discovery — 97
    Yes makes us optimistic — 101
    Yes multiplies happiness — 111
    Yes feeds our creative spirit — 119
    Yes is self-love — 123
    Yes protects us from cynicism — 131
    Yes shows us how powerful we really are — 135

That's all for now! — 141

*"Love is a place
& through this place of
love move
(with brightness of peace)
all places*

*yes is a world
& in this world of yes live
(skillfully curled)
all worlds"*

— e.e. cummings
Poet

The Story of *Yes Changes Everything!*

"You said, remember that life is
Not meant to be wasted
We can always be chasing the sun!
So fill up your lungs and just run
But always be chasing the sun!"

— Sara Bareilles
Singer, Songwriter
From her song, *Chasing the Sun*

There is this amazing story about the day John Lennon and Yoko Ono met: in the Fall of 1966, Yoko was in London for an art exhibition. Already an accomplished avant-garde artist, Yoko was displaying her works at the Indica Gallery as part of an exhibition called *Unfinished Paintings and Objects*.

John visited the gallery the day before the show was scheduled to open. He was skeptical about the displays, and the artist herself, who greeted him with a card that read, literally, "Breathe."

One piece got his attention, though: Yoko had placed a ladder that led up to a canvas on the ceiling on which some tiny type appeared. John had to climb the ladder and look through a small telescope to see what it said.

You might've expected the word to be "love" or "hope," but as John stood there squinting through the magnifying glass on top of that small ladder, he could see that the word was "Yes."

I heard this story a long time ago, and I never forgot it. What does it say about me (maybe about you too 😊) that this story would be so intriguing in the sense of being unique, memorable, thought-provoking?

What is it about *yes* that might matter so much?

Yoko's message

Sometimes I play a game with myself (maybe not a game, more like a spiritual exercise): I ask myself if I knew my life would soon be over, what would be the one or two or 20 things I'd be most mad I didn't accomplish?

Thinking about that list, I ask myself: "Am I making those things, or that one thing, a priority in my life? Am I saying yes to it and concentrating my best energy there?"

It's a great reality check: am I saying yes to the right things in my life? The things that really matter to me and the people I love? Or (more likely when I check-in like this), am I cluttering up my life with a bunch of urgent stuff — the in-my-face unavoidable deadlines of life, the errands I have to run, appointments I need to keep, deadlines I can't avoid — and not focusing on the goals that aren't urgent but definitely important? My beautiful, amazing, super-critical-to-me goals and bucket list?

Like this:

Urgent	Important
Get to work on time	Plan my next career move
Pay bills	Create a savings plan
Fix a cavity	Get teeth cleaned
Make dinner	Plan and buy a week of healthy groceries

The reason I love this reality check is that, like Yoko, I'm learning that what I say yes to is incredibly important, an idea I think her piece was signaling by making yes small and hard to see.

Yes doesn't have to scream — it's that powerful.

How exactly *does* yes change everything?

Yes is a great life strategy. It's a way of looking at what we want to invite into our lives, a way of processing every event and opportunity that comes our way. It's an attitude and a filter. Yes is going into the choices of our lives hope-first, plus smart and sharp.

The yes that changes everything opens the door to amazing. And maybe even more important, it doesn't end there; yes also changes everything that happens afterward. When we say yes, a bunch of serendipitous side effects cascade into our lives:

- We are open, inviting, easy to be around, and counted on to be a constructive voice for other people.
- We're plugged in to what's new and happening, innovations and fresh ideas and discoveries.

- We're energized, on the move, not stagnant in our ideas, jobs, relationships, or joyful pursuits.
- Our minds and hearts are young, flexible, and healthy.
- We're included — maybe even top-of-mind — when anyone (a friend, neighbor, coworker, manager) is thinking of someone for a new project or pursuit because we have a reputation for liking to try new things.
- We're creative and resourceful (because the yes that changes everything is positive, but not always easy!).
- We're never bored — or boring!

What about *The Gift of No*?

How could *Yes Changes Everything!* follow *The Gift of No*, a book I wrote a few years ago about the importance of setting boundaries and saying no with confidence and love? Sounds like a total contradiction!

But *Yes Changes Everything!* is actually a sequel to *The Gift of No*.

That's because the kind of no I wrote about in *The Gift of No* is the healthy no that sets up good, strong boundaries.

It's the no that says, "You really hurt me, and I won't let you do that again."

The no that says, "That's not a subject I'm willing to talk about."

The no that says, "I can't commit to that because if I do, I won't have the energy I need to take care of myself and the people I love," or "I can't make that a priority in my life right now."

That no, the *gift* of no, isn't a rejection of things that are new, fresh, and different in our lives. It doesn't come from cynicism, fear, or anger. The gift of no is a rejection of things that hurt us, that cost us and/or the people we care about, things that put everyone and everything ahead of our own happy/healthy/sane.

That no is a rejection of things we don't want in our lives, the things that don't match our plans or goals or values or passions. Because saying no to what hurts and is unhealthy and depleting is the <u>exact same</u> as saying yes to what's good and right and healthy and positive!

Here's how I wrote about this in *The Gift of No*:

> ...saying no to the things we don't want is EXACTLY THE SAME as saying yes to the things we do want.
>
> By saying no to more time at the office, we say yes to other things we cherish, like long walks at sunset with the dog, an early morning run, or cuddle time with the kids as we read a favorite story together before bed.
>
> By saying no to the low-paying, energy-sapping project we don't want to take on, we free up time to say yes to projects that are interesting, fulfilling, and well-paying.
>
> By saying no to the friend who wants our help (again) with that low-impact, poorly-attended-no-matter-

how-hard-we-try community event, we're saying yes to time working on causes that mean something and can actually have an impact.

Healthy and balanced

Second, in both books, I write about healthy, balanced yeses and healthy, balanced no's. *The Gift of No* has lots of examples of times when saying no is a good idea, but it sure doesn't advocate saying no to everything.

In the same way, saying yes to everything will only make us crazy, broke, exhausted...sometimes all three.

Both extremes can have negative consequences:

- Ruby says yes to every career opportunity, even the ones that don't fit her personality or her dreams.

- After a few bad relationships, Ted swears them off forever.

- Drew wants to get healthier, so he promises himself no more carbs — ever. From now on, it's egg whites, chicken, and spinach every day!

- Bella hates to disappoint people, so she says yes to every demand on her time, no matter how tired she is. She volunteers for everything, and always seems to get tagged for things everyone else turns down.

And you know what, beautiful someone? We can finish every one of these stories, at least generally. These unbalanced yeses and unbridled no's just don't work out:

- Ruby's career goes in directions she never wanted. After about 10 years, she looks around and realizes she's in a job, working for a company, maybe even living in a place she never wanted to be.

- After a year alone, Ted realizes that it made no sense to swear off all relationships, wonders if he's missed out on someone wonderful, says yes without thinking to the next person who looks remotely interesting, has yet another bad experience, and swears off relationships again — this time "really forever," he says.

- Drew stays off carbs for three days, then after a stressful day at work, starved for comfort food, he pulls into a drive-through on the way home. Doesn't love himself afterward.

- One day, Bella picks up her head after slamming back her third espresso to stay awake and finish a project she volunteered for. She wonders whether she's had an actual plan in her entire life, or has she just done what other people wanted her to do? She feels empty and aimless.

Healthy yeses and no's both have boundaries. Boundaries we define based on what matters to us. Boundaries we set up and enforce. And boundaries we lower when (and only if!) we want to. When we decide that the answer is yes, we drop a boundary. When the healthy, balanced answer is no, the boundary stays in place (or maybe we erect a new one!).

So *Yes Changes Everything!* can follow *The Gift of No* because they're really saying the same thing but adding nuance and richer meaning, coming from opposite directions.

In this book, I want us to dive deep and explore the full power of yes in the same way we explored the power of no.

Let's go!

Blue skies to you,
Diana

YES CHANGES EVERYTHING!

DIANA DAVIN

So why <u>not</u> yes?

"Clear your mind of can't."

— Samuel Johnson
English writer

Why don't we say yes to the new, the different, and the unexplored in our lives?

Lots of reasons. Yes is a beginning, the starting point for new experiences and adventures. And for this very reason, yes is a risk. It's a tiptoe (or sometimes a giant leap) into the unknown. Which is why we hang back, or sometimes just run to the safety of no.

And in our hearts we know this.

Saying yes to a relationship, definitely a personal one, but even a work relationship, is also the same as putting our trust on the line. I learned a long time ago (of course the hard way ☺) that when we trust someone, at some point, we *will* get disappointed. It's a given: trust and disappointment go hand-in-hand. We can't say yes to a relationship without the risk of being hurt by it.

More broadly, when we say yes, we worry that accepting the challenge, signing up for the program, or giving of ourselves in a new situation may not work out. We may get embarrassed in front of people.

Yes can also come with losses. We don't want to make the people around us feel alienated — pushed out of our world. If we say yes and step out (i.e., away from them), it's like we're saying that they (and what we have with them) aren't good enough for us. It can seem like we're saying, "I want more than you, than this." It's hard to risk hurting someone like this.

When we reach for something new, we may be afraid of letting go of what we have. We're afraid of no longer fitting in where we're safe and comfortable. Even if it's not great, at least it's familiar. It's not the *unknown*.

Yes also adds to our lives, so we risk being overwhelmed by whatever we're saying yes to. One more thing is going to put us over the top for sure. Beautiful someone, we're not *easily* overwhelmed. We're *legit* overwhelmed! Just a decade ago, the average consumer encountered about 3,000 to 5,000 advertising images a day. Today, that number is between 6,000 and 10,000 a day. It has doubled! We have to tune out some of these and the zillions of other stimuli in our lives just to stay sane!

Um, no
Even when it's exhilarating, yes is new and different, unfamiliar and sometimes scary. It may require new learning and some (maybe a lot) of effort. It can be a lot *easier* to say no, even when saying no isn't *better*.

Maybe we've said yes to new things in the past, set out on a fresh quest, stepped into the unknown — whatever — and things didn't go so well.

Maybe more than once.

And so our natural reaction to any new thing is to say:

- "Um, no. Not going there. Got that lesson already."
- "Fool me once, shame on you; fool me twice, shame on me."
- "The last time I tried something like that, it was an epic fail. I lost a ton of money and wasted a lot of time."

Plus, maybe we're not *un*comfortable. Things may not be great, but they're not awful. They're, you know, okay. Fine. Good enough. No real need for any changes right now.

Sometimes yes is ridiculously scary:

- Taking a new job across the country
- Deciding to hike Machu Picchu
- Starting a brand new relationship
- Going back to school full-time
- Signing (*anything*!) on the dotted line

Could be we're surrounded by negative voices:

- "Look, I know you. You could never…"
- "Um, remember the last time you tried something like that? It wasn't pretty, and I was the one who had to pick up the pieces. You're welcome, by the way."
- "I read this article about someone who [*did whatever you're thinking about*], and they lost everything! Had to move back in with their parents!"

And so, beautiful someone, our world becomes defined by knee-jerk no's:

- "No, I can't."
- "No, I don't."
- "No, I won't."
- "No, it's not possible."
- "No, it's too late."
- "No, you're wrong."
- "No, I'm not ready."
- "No, I could never."
- "No, I'm too [*pick one:* scared/old/young/tall/short/experienced/inexperienced]."

Then maybe:

- "Sounds good, but I tried it once, and it didn't work out."
- "That's gonna take way too long."
- "I'm not into new things at this point in my life."
- "I have enough friends. Don't need new ones."
- "I know somebody who tried that and lost their job!"
- "I'm so exhausted!"
- "I don't have time!"
- "I'd have to have like $30,000 saved to quit my job and try to write a book."
- "No way I could take a HIIT class. I'm just being realistic."
- "No, I haven't asked, I just know that he/she/they/my boss/my family/my friends would never be okay with that."
- "That's fine for other people, but it would never work for me no matter how hard I tried. I just know it."

...and it's back to familiar (safe) ground.

Phew, that was close!

And if you're wondering if it was easy for me to rattle off all these lists of reasons we say no, it was. Because I've said every single one of those things — some of them more than once!

Knee-jerk no's can cost us

Maybe I'm easily overwhelmed, or maybe I (like all of us) am trying to raise my kids, have an actual relationship, spend time with my friends, take care of my house and animals, work, and stay healthy. Saying yes to anything feels like I'm adding to the mountain of stuff I already have to do!

Except, beautiful someone, knee-jerk no's can cost us. And sometimes by the time we realize it, the doors have closed on what would have been a great opportunity, great relationship, or great project, and they are not going to reopen. Regrets? You bet. And for this reason, we can't let knee-jerk no's hold us back and limit our happy, healthy, sane lives.

Yep, knee-jerk no's can cost. Big. Too big.

But not us!

DIANA DAVIN

There's yes...and then there's the yes that changes everything

> "Keep away from people who try to belittle your ambitions. Small people always do that, but the really great make you feel that you, too, can become great."
>
> — Mark Twain
> Humorist and writer

Yes can be the start of adventure and discovery. It can open the door to creativity and optimism. It can be a great way to build our biceps, one labeled *persistence* and the other *determination*.

Can be.

Because there's yes, and then there's the yes that changes everything.

They're not the same.

Yes is just yes. Just acquiescence or even capitulation, giving in or giving up. It can sound like, "Yeah whatever," "Fine, I don't care," "Why not?" "I've got nothing better to do," "Okay, fine!! You win!" or "He/she/they are doing it, so I probably should too."

Imagine the quality of life that results from this kind of decision-making (if we can even call it that!).

On the other hand, the yes that changes everything opens the door to good things. It lets in possibility, renewal, and adventure that together help us build a beautiful, bountiful life — not to mention a happy, healthy, sane one!

The yes that changes everything sounds more like:

> **Adventure** ("So glad I agreed to go on that hike. New Zealand will be amazing!")
> **Affirmation** ("Yes, that's so true!")
> **Agreement** ("LOL, I know. Yeah, totally agree!")
> **Courage** ("I know it's scary, but yeah—I'm going to try anyway. I refuse to be afraid and let that keep me from doing this.")
> **Creativity** ("Well, this is new to me and that part didn't work out, so what else can I try?")
> **Determination** ("I will not give up. I'm going to keep at it! I won't let a bad experience keep me from my dreams.")
> **Inclusion** ("Yes, definitely, you should come with us! We need to talk more.")
> **Optimism** ("It's definitely going to work out. I can make something good happen out of this!")

Sounds amazing! Sign me up, right?
Great, but it's not that simple. We need tools and strategies for putting this quality of yes to work in our lives.

So how do we do more of the good "yes-ing," the type that changes everything, and less (or none!) of the other kind?

It starts with time
Here's a saying (more like a warning ☺) we've heard 1,000 times: "He who hesitates is lost."

It's a way of telling us, "Do it now — right now!" And the implication is clear: "If you wait, things aren't going to go well." As with all sayings like this, the ones deeply embedded in our collective awareness, it's hard to pinpoint its actual origin, but it looks like this particular expression could have been adapted from a line in playwright Joseph Addison's 1712 play Cato: "The woman that deliberates is lost."

Well, thanks for that, Mr. Addison. Without delving into the ridiculous implications about women and thinking, that's still a lot of pressure. The message is that we've got to jump on opportunity, or it will pass us by and never come back.

Even more troubling: the word "lost." Sounds like not just the opportunity, but we are lost. If we do this dangerous thing called "deliberating" for too long, well, that's all she wrote, apparently.

It's true that some opportunities come around once, and if we don't take advantage of them, they pass us by. An out-of-the-blue invitation, a one-of-a-kind special project, a coveted job with an unexpected vacancy because (surprise!) the current occupant took another position.

But most opportunities aren't like this.

Most decisions that we need to make are not in-our-face immediate — we've got days, weeks, or in the case of life partners, mortgages, and careers for example, even years to make a choice. That means if we develop the habit of believing that most of the time, we should jump on stuff without thinking, well, then we definitely are lost. Our lives are defined by impulse, emotion, fear, and other unresourceful feelings and reactions.

On the other hand, if we take the time to deliberate — to think things through — our lives are defined by good choices, including the yes that changes everything. Lots of words go along with this quality of decision-making: facts, experience, judgment...and super-important: *perspective*.

Step back
Perspective is mentally and sometimes even physically standing back from a situation to see it clearly in relation to everything that surrounds it.

Perspective is hard, maybe even impossible, when we're standing six inches from a situation. That's why we've all had the experience of going away on vacation, even just for a weekend, and coming back fresh, with new insights and ideas.

Or going to a good movie, concert, or play and coming back feeling energized.

Or stepping away from our daily life to spend time with great people and having the same experience.

There are lots of reasons why, but one of the main ones is the fresh feeling that comes from space — mental and emotional elbowroom away from our day-to-day routines and chores and obligations. Even changing the air we breathe or the scenery we look at gives us a sense of freshness and renewal.

We feel refreshed, beautiful someone, because our souls naturally want breathing room. Space is organic nutrition to them because they need room to explore and time to understand, to put things in perspective.

Perspective in fine art means depicting elements in a composition that are larger (so they appear closer), smaller (so they appear further away), angled, deep or shallow. It also means being able to see what's approaching and what's receding, all the way to where the lines in a drawing converge and disappear at the "vanishing point." In essence, perspective is the ability to show the relative values of the various elements in a drawing.

In life, perspective helps our minds make distinctions: we can tell whether objects are closer or further away, larger or smaller, approaching us fast or slow. Perspective enables us to know how steep a hill or set of stairs is, how much space there is between cars in the parking lot, even how dense and heavy an object is likely to be if we try to pick it up.

The distinctions that perspective enables us to make can be lifesaving. Think of the depth perception needed to determine the breaking distance between you and the car in front of you, the location and height of a step or bench in the shower, the size of a knife best suited to cut a tomato for salad, and even beyond the visual, our ability to distinguish rotted or poisonous food from edible food. (There is a reason we react the way we do to smelly food!)

Applying this concept to the yes the changes everything is *ka-boom* level powerful: having perspective on a choice is the ability to understand its relative value (importance) in our lives, in the bigger picture, the larger scheme of things, to our future, to the situation, to the people we love. Essentially, what really matters, what totally doesn't…and everything in between. How significant (big) is a choice or outcome or opportunity, especially relative to everything else we can do and need to do?

Having this perspective requires stepping back, getting away from the nose-to-the-subway-train closeness to a decision we're considering so we can tell if saying yes aligns with our goals and values, and how yes could affect the people we love.

It all takes TIME!
So, to get a good view, we need to STEP BACK. Sometimes waaaay back.

Then we need to EVALUATE the situation/opportunity based on our goals and past experiences and COMPARE it to all the other options we have, including doing nothing (always an option, and sometimes a really good one).

Maybe we even need to TALK to people we love and trust about the situation to get their ideas about it, maybe find out if they've had a similar choice to make, what they did, and how it worked out for them.

Couple of good night's SLEEP might be super-helpful too.

Step back.

Compare.

Evaluate.

Talk.

Sleep.

You know where I'm going with this: it all takes TIME!

And to call the time it takes to do all this hesitation, well, whatever. Call it fried green tomatoes — doesn't matter. Just don't call it unnecessary. Or the road to being "lost."

We should never beat ourselves up for taking the time we need to get some perspective and think before jumping into a decision. Taking that time — again, we can call it hesitation — is our brain switching on and our natural self-protective instincts at work. It's our heads saying, "Wait, what?" or "Hold on a second. I need to think about that," or "That may be a great idea, but I'm not sure. I need some time to put it in the mix with all my options."

These aren't the ruminations of someone who is lost. To me they sound like the thoughts of someone who is healthy, strong, and very smart.

Yes is our superpower
Our brains have unlimited capacity for making connections, remembering experiences, and creating beauty. They power everything we think, learn, and feel. They regulate every function in our bodies, voluntary and in-

voluntary — movement, breath, thoughts, heartbeat, and judgment.

Did you know that our brains:

- Can learn seven facts per second
- Contain 100 billion neurons, more than the number of stars in the galaxy
- Operate faster than any supercomputer, forming more than 1 million new connections every day
- Use chemical and electrical signals zipping along billions of neural highways, even when we sleep, at more than 150 miles per hour

That's one amazing supercomputer sitting between our skulls and our chins — and it craves exercise! Which is why there is such a thing as being brain fit.

Have you ever heard the phrase, "Sitting is the new smoking"? Sitting all day long, especially in front of a phone or laptop, strains our hips and backs, weakens our abdominal muscles, tightens our shoulders and pectoral (chest) muscles, and causes us to jut our heads forward, creating neck strain. Being constantly hunched over, usually in a sitting position, takes a tremendous toll on our bodies, head to toe.

Everything hurts because our bodies are literally begging us to get up and move! It's like they're crying: "Exercise me! Strengthen me! Stretch me!" (And we really, beautiful someone, *really* need to listen to them!)

Strength and energy
Importantly, what's true of our bodies is also true of our brains. Routine can be exhausting. When our lives are

filled with predictable schedules and comfort-seeking activities, we feel down, tired, maybe even a little numb.

But when we say yes to something new, suddenly we're filled with vitality, with strength and energy. That's because the supercomputer in our heads is getting exercise: something it craves as much as our bodies do.

When we explore a new hobby, download an app that's going to help us get conversational in a new language to be ready for a trip, or listen to a fast-moving intricate rap song and work hard to decipher the lyrics...all this new sensory input can be tracked in our brains to a series of electrical spikes, and not just one or two, but many neurons, even entire regions of our brains. We're giving our brains a workout!

This activity to tackle and decipher something new, something that stretches us out of comfort zones and away from what's comfortable and familiar generates new brain cells and strengthens the connections between them, is totally energizing. Some science even suggests that mental exercise prevents diseases of the brain such as dementia and Alzheimer's and may even slow the cognitive decline that can happen with age. That may be a long way off for us, but think of the power the yes that changes everything (and the mental workout it gives us) has for our long-term emotional, mental, and spiritual mojo!

The yes that changes everything builds our brain fitness by giving us the challenges we need to stay vital and alive as we explore new cities, hobbies, books, avocations, music, art, careers, ideas, and destinations.

And something else: we need to treat one of the most amazing abilities this organic computer in our heads gives us — the ability to choose yes — like the superpower it is.

Space in our lives is a <u>privilege</u>

When we think about what saying yes can do in our lives, everything that it can introduce and enable and create and inspire, it's easy to see that the ability to choose yes really is a superpower that needs to be treated like one. We can't just throw the door open, say yes, and let anything saunter into our lives unexamined and unchecked.

Instead, we need to respect that when we choose to say yes, we are literally opening the door wide to let experiences and people and opportunities into our lives — that's a sacred space that they are entering! Being part of our lives is a *privilege*. That's not to sound arrogant; it's just to acknowledge that in order to stay healthy and happy and free to care for and contribute to our families, friends, jobs, communities (not to mention ourselves!), we need to view our lives as precious.

To start, this means the yes that changes everything has got to check three boxes:

- ☑ It has to fit our **plans and values**.
- ☑ It must have a **positive purpose**.
- ☑ It needs to be **right for us** and the people we care about — right now.

☑ The yes that changes everything fits our plans and values

Where do you want your life to go?

The yes that changes everything depends on knowing.

Because when we know where we want our lives to go, we can respond to good opportunities by saying things like: "That's been a goal of mine for a while, so I think it would be great for me to go after," and "Sounds really good! I've always been fascinated by that idea!" and "I think that could work really well for my family," and "I've always wanted to go back to school, so that sounds super-interesting."

On the other hand, when we're tempted to say yes to a choice that doesn't line up with our plans and priorities, we can say with confidence:

- "That's not something I'm interested in."
- "I can't make that a priority."
- "No thanks. I'm working on a really important goal right now, so I don't have the time."

Happy, healthy, sane living lines up with our values and goals. The reverse is also true: when we don't live in this kind of alignment, we're all kinds of miserable. So let's go there, beautiful someone.

To start us off, have a quick read of these real people and their stories:

A businessowner who cares deeply about relationships has alienated many people to build her career, including her husband and her closest friends. *Lonely* doesn't even come close to describing how she feels.

A physician who went into medicine at his family's urging feels little connection or compassion for his patients. His real passion: his heritage apple orchard filled with heirloom trees. His face lights up when he talks about it.

An attorney has built a practice that puts such demands on her time that community service and volunteer work — activities that once gave her a great sense of connection and significance — are out of the question. She's making great money but would trade it all for the sense of happiness and fulfillment she used to have.

Listen for an important shared characteristic: regardless of their financial success and no matter what profession they're in, these people's lives aren't lined up with one of their most important values. And when heart and hands don't match — when what we bring into our lives (what we say yes to) causes us to ignore something we truly value — our happy/healthy/sane takes a major hit.

What matters to you?
- What causes (the environment, human rights, elder care, literacy...) are important?
- What spiritual beliefs and practices?
- What uses of your free time (exercise, meditation, volunteering, artwork...)?

- What qualities in your relationships (honesty, loyalty, commitment, communication, personal space...)?
- What quality of work experience (work/life balance, working for nice people, financial rewards/benefits, hyper-challenge, a genuinely supportive environment...)?

The yes that changes everything considers these priorities in advance:

- Yes to volunteer work should line up with the causes that truly matter to you.
- Yes to a time-intensive commitment at work or home might seriously infringe on time to paint or write.
- Yes to a project for someone with poor communication skills will probably be stressful.
- Yes to a job that pays well but will in all likelihood drain everything out of you will compromise your value of good work/life balance.
- Yes to a job for a new company that's a lateral move may have good upward mobility but won't provide the kind of financial boost usually associated with job changes.

And <u>who</u> matters to you?

- Who do you love?
- Who depends on you?
- Who are you a role model for?

The yes that changes everything factors in these people and their needs:

- Yes to a new job will impact the people who depend on you.
- Yes to an ethical choice will affect the people you influence.
- Yes to a time commitment will affect your availability to the people you love.
- Yes to traveling for a holiday to visit family will affect the amount of time and energy you have for other people who may want to spend time with you.
- Your choices — what you agree to — as a manager or leader will affect the people who report to you.

When we know what matters to us, our yeses, when we use them, are aligned with who and what we value. They feel right, healthy, and positive.

These are the yeses with the power to change everything.

☑ The yes that changes everything has a positive purpose

Think of a buffet filled with freshly-made food: crisp veggies, grilled chicken and fish, salad, and whole grain bread, but also creamy pasta salads, saucy wings, fried everything, and buttery garlic bread. Self-serve! We get to spoon whatever we want onto our plates. We're choosing what we want, *what we say yes to.*

This is life itself, beautiful someone! When we say yes to something, what we're really saying is, "I'm going to let that into my life," whether that's mouth food, brain food (thoughts, information, advice, inspiration), or whole body food (the experiences that shape our lives and who we become)...all of which we "consume" in one way or another. Saying yes to anything, including ideas, relationships, opinions, jobs, leisure activities, and plans is saying, "I believe this is worthy of space in my one precious head, heart, body, and life."

Short term, long term, or permanently, one of the key differences between any-old-yes and the yes that changes everything is positive purpose that makes whatever we're letting in worthy of space in our lives.

Positive purpose makes for a yes that changes everything by nourishing us with thing like:
- Respect for the priorities of our lives
- Added value to our jobs and relationships
- Forward movement — progress and growth
- Inspiration that we then use to positively influence ourselves and other people

- Improvements in our lives and the lives of the people around us
- Good health
- Strength
- Education and information
- A sense of pride
- New directions that expand our minds and hearts

Back to our buffet

The yes that can change everything is the good food: the salad, grilled chicken, whole-grain bread, and other foods we can put on our plates that are nutritious and filling, food that not only sustains us for today, but protects us from the harmful effects of unhealthy fats, refined sugars, and simple carbs. These are the yeses — the choices with positive purpose that nourish us — that change everything.

With this in mind, there are areas in our lives where we should always err on the side of yes — any choice that nourishes our:

- Hopes and dreams
- Authentic, whole selves
- Genuine love (in all its forms)
- Good physical health
- Good emotional/spiritual health
- Good influence—a positive legacy for the people who look up to us
- Ability to be a blessing in any situation
- Heartfelt causes we believe in and know in our souls are truly important and valuable
- Ability to speak up when it matters

- Life balance — not allowing anything to take over so much of our energy that we can't bring our best to it

Tuning out the naysayers
- "What makes you think you could ever…?"
- "Look, I know you. I know what you're capable of, and this definitely isn't it."
- "Hey, I knew you when you couldn't even spell. You're gonna go for a Master's?"
- "I never did that, and I survived! What, you're so much better than me?"
- "Why do you need a bigger house? Just be glad you have a roof over your head at all."
- "You should stick with what you know."
- "You? Really?" (*condescending chuckle plus eye roll*)

Sometimes it's like all we have to do is mention an exciting goal, and the naysayers start in like this. Maybe they tried the same thing, it didn't work out, and they want to help us avoid the pain they went through. They're actually trying to help.

From discouraging...
Sometimes, honestly? Not so much. They may be afraid of being left behind, of our lives outpacing theirs somehow. Afraid of change, of the unknown and what it might do to them personally.

Then there are naysayers who think cynicism makes them look smart. They're skeptical from the get-go: "What? How could that possibly work?" "I read an article about someone who tried that and lost everything!" They dig and dig until aha! they find the tragic flaw in your dream: "Okay, so I finally figured out what's wrong with your idea!" (as if we're supposed to be happy about that).

Naysaying can be especially discouraging when it's coming from influential people in our lives.

Or when it's coming nonstop at the speed of light.

When it's cynicism disguised as "reason."

When it reminds us of our less-than-stellar past.

When it cherry picks bad headlines for reasons we shouldn't try.

...to positive!
Naysayers can have their opinions (they always seem to have lots of them 😊), but let's leave them out of our awesomeness. The real danger is that if we listen to them, our yeses can start to seem ridiculous. Psychologist and author Piero Ferrucci once wrote, "How often — even before we began — have we declared a task 'impossible'? ...A great deal depends on the thought patterns we choose and on the persistence with which we affirm them."

This is why, if we talk to anyone who's achieved the "impossible" (dream job, dream project, dream goal), there's no question that their own positive purpose gave them energy and determination to tune out the naysayer chorus of "No," "Can't," "Don't," and "No way!" And their ability to do so was as important to their victory as anything they actually *did*.

Positive purpose — the certainty that what they had said yes to and were determined to achieve was good and worthy of space in their lives — gave them the resilience and confidence to answer the naysayers with an empowered:

- "Yup, me!"
- "You bet!"
- "Oh, that's yesterday's story. I'm better prepared now."
- "It's a new day!"
- "Yeah, but I know better now."
- "...." (*i.e., nothing at all*)

So, next time we hear:

- "No one's ever done it before," let's think: "So, I'll be the first. I'm a trailblazer!"
- "People have tried that and failed," let's say: "But I haven't tried it yet, and I won't fail because I will make it work."
- "It can't be done," let's know: "All I needed for inspiration was one example of someone who succeeded at this to know — it can be done. And I've got that."

The juice

Positive purpose also gave achievers the juice to push past obstacles and reach the finish line on their yeses. It gave them the determination to keep plugging away. When opportunity didn't knock, it gave them the energy to build a door:

- Make the call
- Send the note

- Step up and volunteer
- Introduce themselves
- Take the initiative to network with great people
- Call in favors

Positive purpose enabled them to surround themselves with people who had faith in them.

It enabled them to say yes and then ask, "Okay, so…

- "How can I…"
- "What should I do to get ready to…"
- "What are the best ways to…"
- "Who can help me, and how can I return the favor?"
- "What are some of the pitfalls to avoid as I try this?"
- "What did I learn from the last time I tried something like this?"
- "Who do I know who did this already and what would I want to ask this person?"

And when they weren't feeling strong, positive purpose helped them let the dream take a little nap, confident they'd wake up refreshed and ready to take it on again soon.

☑ The yes that changes everything is right for us and the people we care about — right now

Yes can only change everything — it only has that power — when the timing is right to open the door in our lives to an experience, person, idea, or choice. When the timing is right, yes does its magic: it changes us in good ways.

Dream Come True includes a section I called, "Is this right, right now?" I think some of it applies to the yes that changes everything:

> I don't know if timing is everything as the saying goes, but I do know that the difference between the right and the not-quite-right time to go after a dream can make a huge difference. When the timing is right...
>
> You feel ready and open to new people, ideas, and experiences. You're feeling strong and confident, sending out good energy that's coming right back at you in the form of positive experiences and people.
>
> You've thought about the costs and risks—financial, emotional, personal—of pursuing this dream, and they're manageable and worth it. You're not putting everything financially or emotionally on the line.
>
> You're feeling physically and emotionally strong. You're not trying to deal with health issues, family problems, huge, non-stop demands on your time, or big life changes at the same time.

You've thought about if and how your dream come true will affect the most important people in your life. You've talked to them about it, heard them out, and fully understand how they feel.

You've shared the dream with friends and/or mentors in your life, the people whose opinions you really value.

You've talked to people who've succeeded at what you're trying to do and gotten honest feedback from them.

For sizeable dreams, you're plugged in to how radical a change living this dream or reaching this goal might be.

If you dream about moving to a rural area to start a small farm, you've thought through not only what this will mean from a work perspective but from a quality of life perspective (e.g., driving 30 minutes for a latte, feelings of isolation, pitch black nights, no more sidewalks or streetlamps...)

If you want a high-end sales position, you've thought about the toll travel will take on you and your family and you're okay with leaving backyard picnics on Sunday afternoons to go to the airport and fly across the country for a Monday morning meeting.

If you dream of owning a townhouse in the 'burbs, you've thought through how different this will be from renting in the city and are ready to fix your own faucets.

For smaller dreams, you know you've got the bandwidth to go after them: you can take two hours at night for an online creative writing course after you put the kids to bed—and have good energy to get the most out of it. Or you've researched what's involved in running a cancer fundraiser in your town. You know you could put in the time and energy, and you know at least two other people who'd be all-in to help you if you went for it.

But you know what, beautiful someone? The yes that changes everything is even bigger than our dreams. It touches *every* choice, *every* decision, *every*thing we let into our lives: ideas, relationships, opportunities, day-to-day choices. So while a key part of our choice to say yes is timing, unlike our long-terms dreams, we need to decide whether to choose yes *every day*, many times a day.

Is it the right time to let that person in? To say yes to that trip? To follow that person? To make those plans for Friday? To invest in that property? To take on that project?

For any choice, think about checking some or all of these boxes:

- ☐ I feel ready to be open to this person, idea, or opportunity.

- ☐ I know the costs and risks — financial, emotional, personal — of the choice to say yes right now.

- ☐ In this moment, I feel physically and emotionally strong. I'm not dealing with health issues, family problems, huge demands on my time, or big life changes.

- ☐ I've thought about if and how the choice to say yes will affect the most important people in my life.

- ☐ I've shared this choice with friends other people whose opinions matter to me.

- ☐ I've researched/thought through the longer-term impact saying yes to this idea or opportunity will have.

Now, step back and think it through: what boxes could you check? How important are the ones you couldn't?

Is this yes right, right now?

YES CHANGES EVERYTHING!

Making room for *yes!*

> "Turn your face to the sun and the shadows fall behind you."
>
> — Maori Proverb

There won't be room for anything fresh and new in our lives if they're full of stuff that shouldn't be yeses for us anymore — things that are just plain clutter for us now.

A cluttered life is too busy with burdens and preoccupations to even think about introducing anything new. There's too much going on, never mind that lots of it isn't helping us move our lives ahead in positive directions!

Clutter is a monster obstacle to a happy, healthy, sane life, and it stands solidly in the way of yes. Clutter is things we no longer want, can't use, or have three of already. It's anything we've been done with for a while...the car (relationship, job, living situation) that's broken down on the side of the road that we haven't hopped out of yet.

Once we decide we want to make room for yes, for freshness and emotional, physical, spiritual space, <u>it's time to let go of clutter</u>. We need to open up space for inspiration, hope, and beauty — a fresh new sense of life.

I always say that one of the best gifts we can give anyone is a box of contractor bags — the really thick ones that you can fill and fill, and they never break. As the junk goes from our closets and garages into them, we look around at the open space, the clean lines, the simplicity!

Ahhhh! Breathing room!

Let's do it!
Pull a contractor bag out of the box and give it a few sharp shakes. There, it's open. Oooh, it's big! What should we drop into it?

Let's start with the tangibles, things that are concrete and visible, by asking ourselves: "Are these things useful and healthy for me to have in my life?"

...or do we look at them and think:

- "I don't even care about this. It's just one more thing I've got to insure, dust off, worry about, and pack up next time I move."
- "I forgot I even had this."
- "I haven't used this in a year."
- "I've never even worn this...the tag is still on!"
- "Oh, that salesperson really convinced me to get this."
- "I have two (or 20) of these."
- "This is literally falling apart."
- "These sandals only go with one pair of shorts I own."
- "This never fit right."
- "I liked this until I brought it home; it looked way better in the store."
- "Um, what was I thinking?"

Next up: the sneaky stuff

So those are the tangibles — the things we can see and feel. Things we can literally, physically drop into a bag and toss or donate.

Sneaky clutter is the *in*tangibles: things we can't see our touch but that are slowing us down and blocking the way forward as surely as a pile of bricks.

Beautiful someone, in our happy, healthy, sane lives, there's **no room** for a relationship that works only when we compromise our true selves.

No room for a job that doesn't meet our goals or, worse, one that makes us so miserable (so, so, *so* miserable) that we have to drag ourselves to it every day.

No room for ideas that aren't full of optimism and potential.

No room for regret.

No room for resentment and unforgiveness.

So let's open another contractor bag — a symbolic one this time — and drop in the intangibles that need the heave-ho to make room for our happy life of yes:

- The job or career that no longer excites or challenges us
- The friendship that hasn't felt good in a really long time
- The goal that once seemed worth pursuing, but no longer does
- Knee-jerk reactions and opinions that we haven't questioned in a long time

- Holidays and other occasions we always agree to do but dread every minute leading up to them
- Unhealthy habits that we should have quit a long time ago
- Anything we've "always done a certain way" that needs a reboot (eating habits, exercise routines, types of books, movies, and music that we've always listened to...)

This isn't easy! There's lots of thinking involved — we don't want to ditch too early on a goal.

Or end a long-term relationship just because it's hit a bumpy spot.

Or question our spiritual beliefs because of a brief period of disillusionment.

And changing habits and old ways of thinking is just super-hard to begin with.

But sometimes, we know it's time to ditch:

- The role model that's proven over and over not to be one
- The job we should have left years ago because it's just safe and nothing more
- The vacation plans that just bore us with their predictability so that we come back home afterward, not feeling energized and fresh, but somehow more tired than when we left
- The relationship that's not growing and just makes us feel sad
- The friends who we can't be honest and real around

- The friends who always seem to make us feel bad, unless we're making them happy, often at our own expense
- The goal that's taken so much from us without giving back that even the possibility of reaching it isn't thrilling anymore
- The goal that's costing us (financially, spiritually, physically) more than it will ever give back, and when we look at people who've achieved this goal, we don't actually want to be like them
- The degree we went after because our parents/friends/professors/Aunt Sarah thought would be great for us, but it isn't — it really isn't

Let's get more specific...

Opinions in need of a *huh?*
Sometimes we've had a certain point of view for so long that it feels like hardened cement, heavy and immovable. It's like we don't hold this opinion, but instead, it holds us. Beautiful someone, we never want to feel this way in our happy, healthy, sane lives!

Hardened and immovable ideas and opinions are a recipe for isolation and resentment, anger and frustration. Because having opinions that have been entrenched in us for years, that don't change no matter how much we've learned and grown and experienced since we first held them, isn't healthy. Everything about us, including our points of view, must evolve and grow.

Think of how refreshing it is to feel like your mind has been opened and you can say, "Oh my gosh, I never even thought of it that way! That's an excellent point!"

You've gained a new perspective and opened a door in your mind and your soul.

So let's go there with some deep-dish questions:

- "Are there ideas or opinions I've held for so long that I haven't reexamined in a long time?"
- "When someone questions my points of view, is my immediate reaction to get annoyed?"
- "Do I react to new ideas with instant skepticism?"
- "Does everything seem like a simple yes/no choice?"

If these questions make us wiggle a little in our seats, that's good! Sometimes positive change does that! So is it time for a reboot in some of your thinking?

Grudges

Forgiveness is a process of letting go of past hurts that takes time. We can release those hurts right away through sheer willpower, but, beautiful someone, moving on is a process, and we need to be gentle with ourselves. We're not machines with on/off switches, and pain takes its time.

Still, and I say this gently and with great respect for your pain: grievances are clutter taking up space in our souls and blocking the yes that changes everything. When we hold on to them, think about them, remember them, sort through them like we can figure out why (why? *why?!*) they happened. When we worry about whether the offender is suffering (most likely, they are not), these grievances are holding us back.

YES CHANGES EVERYTHING!

From *Dream Come True*:

> ...beautiful someone, I say from my heart to yours: forgiveness is some the hardest work we will ever—ever—do, but it's also some of the most important for dreamers like us. It lets us drop the bricks in our pockets and move forward.
>
> Personal detail: I'm so serious about the importance of forgiveness that I have, inked on my arm for life, these lines from poet e.e. cummings:
>
> *let it go*
> *let them go*
> *let all go*
> *so comes love*
>
> ...when—and only when—we let it all go, we can love, dream, beautify, share, and in all ways, create our lives.
>
> ...and when you're free from anger and resentment, rising above and then zipping past all those bricks on the way to your dream, you realize something incredibly important:
>
> ***Forgiveness is something you do for yourself.***

Two choices

Full disclosure: dropping old grievances is something I've had to work on a lot. I have this childish sense of fairness and fair play that takes a major hit whenever someone does something hurtful or selfish or outright cruel. And the injustice doesn't even have to be directed at me. Could be at anyone, even something I've seen on the news. It's like I can't let it go (forgive) until they a.) fess up to what they did, b.) admit that it was wrong, and c.) ask for forgiveness.

We have some years of experience between us beautiful someone, you and I, so let me ask: how often does someone who's upset us go through a.), b.), and c.)? Let's just say in my own experience I wouldn't need to use too many fingers to count the number of times. And interesting, as we stew over old offenses, often the guilty party bounces along, either oblivious to what s/he's done or truly without conscience about it.

This means we have two choices: hold on to the hurt and let it clutter up our lives and sap the energy we could use for the good stuff, for yes.

Or — let it go to free up our thought calories for positive possibility and create space for the yes that changes everything.

And this is true whether the person "deserves" to be forgiven or not.

Because in the end, forgiveness doesn't make the other person right.

It makes us free.

Sweet fragrance
I love the way author Mark Twain described forgiveness when he wrote: "Forgiveness is the fragrance that the violet sheds on the heel that has crushed it."

Sounds dramatic, but it's true in a couple of ways: like the flower emitting a beautiful fragrance after being crushed, forgiveness is a miracle. In our cause-and-effect world, forgiveness is the opposite of what should be expected after an offense.

It doesn't make sense.

What makes more sense: "You hurt me so I should hurt you back." Forgiving someone instead of striking back is a surprise. And in that surprise, there is a moment, a breath, a new chance. We ditch the heaviness of resentment, bitterness, and anger, and we make room for yes.

When we see someone who seems to be walking around carting all the offenses in their lives behind them like so many bricks in a wagon, they are anything but happy and anything but sane or healthy.

First of all, they can't go very far — it's hard to move when they're carting all those bricks everywhere.

Second, they're emotionally exhausted from trying to remember the reasons and circumstances that created each brick and keep tabs on who's on their good list or bad list. Who's dropped a brick in their wagon? When? How big was the brick? Has the brick-dropper suffered from guilt and other appropriate punishments?

Third, and super-important for the yes that changes everything, someone who carts the offenses in their lives around with them tends to say no to new things because, well, their wagon's already so full of old offenses and junk that there's no room for anything new.

They don't focus on the future because they're so busy being preoccupied and weighed down by the past. And as they try to polish the bricks in their wagon, keeping them fresh by remembering every one of them in detail, on some level they realize a brick is just a brick and always will be. So they don't tend to feel very accomplished or positive about how they're spending their time — they're just polishing bricks after all.

Space for yes!

It's a memorable image: holding on to offenses, carting the burden of anger around everywhere, re-living the pain every time some remark or situation reminds them of what happened, and polishing things that will always be dull and ugly…all this just keeps them not just stuck in the past, but in the worst of the past.

Beautiful someone, we all have a long list of offenses we suffered at the hands (and mouths!) of yet another long list of culprits. We could all take out our lists and go over them with each other to compare notes. Which offenses were the worst? Whose list is the longest?

But that wouldn't change anything.

It would only renew the anger we felt when the stuff first happened to us, no matter how long ago that was.

We'd just feel horrible all over again. There would be no chance of a fresh start without this offense weighing us down.

And less room for yes.

But if we forgive, cross the offense off our list (or better yet, not even keep a list), we can let go of the anger, free of it for good and ready to move on to better things. We can dump our bricks in a pile on the side of the road, and sprint ahead with an empty wagon, full of space for yes.

Right about now, you're remembering a particular hurt and thinking, "Impossible! After what she did? No way!" but forgiveness doesn't have to be a feeling; it can be a decision, and that decision doesn't have to be supported by our feelings right away. We can give ourselves the time we need for that.

Be gentle and kind to yourself, beautiful. Don't wait for your feelings to change to drop the heavy burden of old offenses. Decide to forgive — for your own sake — and just think of what you'll do with all that energy freshly channeled into *yes*.

...but maybe not so much forget
We always hear the phrase "forgive and forget," but I'm not sure I'm capable of that kind of sainthood. I also think this is a kind of trap because does "forgive and forget" mean that if we can't forget an offense — like totally, completely, and forever delete it from our brain's hard drive — we're not actually forgiving the person for doing it? Because I've forgiven (at least I hope I have) a lot of hurts I still remember pretty clearly.

The Gift of No covers how healthy boundaries enable us to choose no when doing so keeps us, and the people we love, safe and sane. How without boundaries, we're compromising the sanctity of our lives and our bodies.

Healthy boundaries protect our dreams and goals by making them important in our lives and turning away requests, opportunities, invitations, even phone calls that infringe on our true priorities.

Healthy boundaries make the people we love (including ourselves ☺) priorities in our lives. Often those boundaries are decisions, they are the word "no" coming from us directed to a boundary-crashing person or incident in the making. But sometimes boundaries need to be physical. We need to put physical space between ourselves and a boundary crasher. This kind of boundary can be especially effective when it comes to forgiveness.

What I'm saying is that forgiveness doesn't mean trusting someone who's been undependable, unpredictable, or disloyal to us in the past. It doesn't mean allowing ourselves to be taken advantage of or taking the blame for something we didn't do. And it definitely doesn't mean putting ourselves physically in the same situation again with a repeat offender, knowing the same thing is pretty likely to happen and hurt us again when it does. Sometimes, it's not a good idea to restore a relationship with someone who's proven to be a boundary crasher with recidivism issues.

Forgiveness means letting go of the hurt, not thinking about it, not re-living it 100 times by talking about it to other people, and staying away, *sometimes far away*, from repeat offenders. Importantly this is not an aggressive shove, but a peaceful detachment from them.

And while I absolutely believe in second chances — everyone is entitled to bad day, a bad week, even a bad month, and we need to cut them some slack — I also firmly believe poet Maya Angelou's sage advice, "When someone shows you who they are, believe them."

Worn out ways of thinking

Old ways of thinking are clutter in our lives too, blocking the yes that changes everything.

Regret

Let's start with regret. Regret is a type of guilt, which is something that absolutely doesn't belong in our happy, healthy, sane lives. Regrets are things we're sorry for. Mistakes we think we've made. Chances we didn't take. Opportunities we jumped on that didn't go so well. Things we blurted out at the wrong moment. Things we didn't say. People we trusted that we shouldn't have. Job choices we made that wasted our time.

Regrets are a huge form of clutter that's even more sneaky precisely because we don't think of them as clutter. But regrets are an obstacle as real as a stone wall that stands in the way of yes.

The heavy guilt of regret makes us hesitate to say yes. It damages our judgment and self-trust. It makes us think we don't deserve good in our lives — so new opportunities, people, experiences? "Um, no. Because, well I regret some mistakes I made in the past..." (just like the other 8 billion people on the planet, beautiful someone ☺!).

The frame we put around any situation fills with a matching image. This means that if we call something a *mistake*, regrets will fill the frame.

So let's reframe it!

The truth is that every situation that leads to regret *is also one we learned from*. Not only does this way of thinking about them take the sting out of these situations, it lets us look forward with hope rather than back with regret. If we learned from it, we're already thinking about applying those lessons in the future.

From *regret* to *lesson*.

One small wording change, and boom baby! From clutter that's holding us back and crowding out yes, to good information that jets us forward — smarter than we were before.

Oh yeah!

Our "mistakes"

Take a look back over the last five years. Whether things have changed a little or a lot, we've come a long way. People have come and gone — friends, romances, bosses, maybe jobs. Roommates, apartments, houses too.

And it's because of these changes that we know more: what works and what doesn't in our lives. What we like, and what we don't. Who we're attracted to...and not.

Here's a (very partial) list of lessons I've learned from my "mistakes" over the last five years:

- Fear is not a good motivator for me.
- I can be too trusting too early in a relationship.
- I get intellectually depressed if my brain isn't challenged — often and a lot.

- I tend to compare myself to outside standards that aren't even real — I kind of make them up and set them at perfection-level, whether that's cooking dinner, writing books, raising my kids, or literally anything else!

Okay your turn, beautiful. What's on your list of lessons from the last five years?

And now, every time we say, "I wish that had gone better," we can just add something new to our list of stuff we've learned to use next time.

We've handed ourselves another chance to tackle a situation or make a choice. To reinvent it this time. To return from the next battle, a little worn and weary, but definitely smarter. To do this thing better, with more kindness and empathy. And to grow.

It's a new beginning, a new yes.

Comparison

Next up: comparison. In *Dream Come True*, I wrote about something I call The Comparison Game, the incredible burden of comparing ourselves to other people:

> We spend waaay too much time looking at everyone else, reading about "overnight" successes (who have almost always worked 10 years behind the scenes before getting their big break), about prodigies and instant billionaires.
>
> Then, after packing all this into our brains and hearts, we innocently take a look in the mirror and see...what exactly? Truth. Ourselves. Our beautiful, hardworking,

honest, naked selves. How—HOW can this compare to the well-written headlines, gorgeous photography, and carefully edited stories showcasing the best of the best and making dream-reaching look so easy and instant in 100 words or less?

The problem is, we're looking at other people's outsides with our insides. It's apples and oranges! We're comparing the naked truth about ourselves to other people's made-for-primetime stories! You see? Apples and oranges! Or more like refrigerators and sunscreen: NOTHING in common.

...Here's the truth—and please remember this one down in your beautiful bones—we are different. That's it. That's the reason comparison is such a game in the first place. We are each as unique as our fingerprints, and so comparison, in a very real way, is ridiculous.

...the Comparison Game is a mediocrity magnet that dream seekers have to resist with everything we've got. It is the status quo's most useful weapon, a tiny seed of "You are weird" and "Be ashamed of your out-of-the-box ideas" and "You want to try WHAT?" that takes root if we water it with belief, time, and attention.

Beautiful someone, we're not better or worse than anyone else. We're different from everyone else! This is the real sneaky part of The Comparison Game and a huge way in which it blocks the yes that changes everything. Comparison encourages us to be the *same* — to ditch the yes that changes everything in favor of the yeses that make us cookie-cutter identical to everyone around us.

How can that be good?

If we are creating ourselves by looking at everyone else and making our choices based on theirs, we will all end up looking exactly the same. ("Number 12 Looks Just Like You" is an episode of the original *Twilight Zone* about this. It's based on "The Beautiful People," a fable by Charles Beaumont about a girl in a futuristic society where everyone has plastic surgery to look identical — seriously creepy, but unforgettable and worth watching!)

And with all this shape-shifting ourselves to be just like everybody else, there's absolutely no room for the yes the changes everything for us and the people we love in our one-of-a-kind lives. We thrive as individuals, as families, as communities, and as a world based on our uniqueness as individuals coming together to create something bigger and better (and definitely more interesting!) as a whole.

Worry

Next up: worry. So, we're going to worry. It's just part of being alive and involved in life — in a relationship, career, house, body, family — there's a lot to worry about. But what if we thought about it this way:

> **It's not worth worrying about things we *can* change because we can take action to change them.** We can do things to influence them to move in the direction we want them to go. So instead of worrying, we can simply take action and know that we're doing everything we can to move these things in a good direction.

It's not worth worrying about the things we *can't* change because we can't do anything about them: the weather, interest rates, other people's choices and behavior… So, if we can't do anything to change them, it's pointless to worry about them.

It's a way of thinking about *The Serenity Prayer* by theologian Reinhold Niebuhr: "God, grant me the serenity to accept the things I cannot change, the courage to change the things I can, and the wisdom to know the difference."

Now if you knew me personally, you'd be on the floor right now, laughing so hard. *Because I am the OG worrywart.* I can sometimes stay up all night worrying about everything, anything…it doesn't really matter what, just a bunch of things that rotate in the carousel of my mind.

To wit: one night not long ago, I couldn't sleep because I was worried that I couldn't find my right clog. *My right clog.* Where had I left it? It's from the only pair of clogs I own, and I wear them every day. They're Dansko, translation: not cheap. If I couldn't find the right clog, well the left all by itself wasn't going to do me any good. I'd have to buy a new pair, which was something I couldn't drop $150 on right then. So I literally worried about finding my right clog.

Then the carousel in my head rotated to jury duty. I'd been called and already postponed twice, so I had to go. But of course my jury service date fell on the same day I was able to schedule a meeting with a book publishing genius who I had been dying to meet who had like zero availability. What to do, what to do, what to do?

Then the carousel rotated again, and next up was —

"Okay, okay, okay — I get it!" I hear you scream. (I feel for you, I really do, beautiful someone.)

The point is, I may sound very philosophical about worry, but I am *not*.

One thing that does work for me though: *action and more action*. I do feel better when I am taking action on something, whether it's something I'm worried about or a goal I'd like to achieve. As long as I am moving, I can't worry about the things I can't change.

My motto: "The only thing I can absolutely control is how hard I work."

When I know I'm taking action to move the things I *can* change in a good direction, I just sleep better. The carousel in my head rotates with puppies and rainbows.

So maybe let's just rename worry to action planning — you and me Superperson, let's go!

And finally: approval seeking (or: "Whose mirror is it anyway?")
Getting dressed in the locker room before class, I overhear two women joking about someone who's wearing some seriously bright workout clothes. "I want one of those mirrors," one says with a smirk, "the kind that makes her think that outfit looks good."

I'm aware — the whole gym is aware — of who they're talking about. She's tall, maybe six feet, and super strong. In the weight room, she moves without a word, picking up huge dumbbells and pumping lots of plates. Afterward, she and her neon tangerine leggings and chartreuse tank top stroll into the studio for a group class. She walks confidently across the floor, head high, shoulders back. Her eyes are clear, her expression open and softly smiling.

Looking at her, I get a little misty-eyed. "I want to be like that. How do you get like that?" I wonder. "Do you just wake up one day after years of professional-grade wall flowering and think, 'Screw it. I'm curvy, I like myself, and I'm going to do, say, and wear what I want'? Or are you born thinking that way? And if you don't have that kind of confidence by the time you're 30, can you get it? Hypnosis maybe? Meds? What is *wrong* with me?"

Because I believe that woman had it right. She liked what she saw in the mirror, and what she knew was under her clothes...herself. Maybe what she was doing was more important than what she was wearing. Maybe she was proud of herself for being able to buy the outfit after saving up for it. Maybe it made her feel a certain way that enabled her to be so confident and self-assured.

Maybe many things.

But you know, big picture, this really didn't have anything to do with whether her outfit worked. It had to do with how she felt, how she carried herself. The high probability that she knew what people were thinking and didn't care. The fact that she probably felt beautiful (focused, powerful, confident) and that for her, that feeling was deeply private and personal. That she only looked in her own mirror and knew her beauty was in the eye of one beholder — herself. No one else's opinion mattered. It was her mirror after all.

When we start to embrace the yes that changes everything, we will start businesses and take on projects people will say we have no rational reason to attempt. We will try and fail, and others will point to these situations as clear (sometimes even "spiritual") reasons we should stop. We will believe in ourselves way beyond the point everyone else has given up on us, underestimated us, lost confidence in us, and said things like, "You mean you haven't finished that yet?" and "Maybe it's just not meant to be," and "You know, there *is* such a thing as a bad idea."

Just in a purely literal sense, the yes that changes everything has to be different, it has to stand out, otherwise it isn't going to change anything.

Approval seeking is like next-level Comparison Gaming where we're looking right and left for cues in terms of our standards of what's good and right and valuable. It's even more harmful though because it puts us in the position of trying to stand in the ever-shifting sands of other people's opinions.

And if we want to really add to the crazy-making emotional and spiritual clutter of approval seeking, we can acknowledge that sometimes we're seeking the approval of a bunch of people who don't even agree with each other! It would be easier to take our souls and drop them into a Cuisinart set to julienne.

What You Think of Me Is None of My Business

So public speaking is hard, a fact I can state from lots of experience. And it takes a while to get comfortable with it. Except for a very small number of people who are born with the gift, the only thing that gets us past the crippling stage fright and pounding hungry dragonflies in our guts is experience. You just have to get up there and do it, sometimes shaking and sputtering and dry mouthed, but you just have to do it.

Somewhere along the line though, you do get comfortable. You do. At least that's been my trajectory with it. I'm comfortable now, but I remember all too well the early years when I used 100 tricks to look more comfortable than I felt (which was not at all), like keeping a Beany Baby in my pocket to squeeze while I talked. Wearing something with pockets so I could put my hands in them to hide the fact that they were visibly shaking. Wearing glasses instead of contacts which somehow gave me something to hide behind. Using lots of visual aids to give the audience something to look at so they would *just stop staring at me!*

But by far one of the most important things that you have to get over in public speaking is caring what people think. Because I'll tell you that you'll be standing up there and you'll see people (some of them in the very first row) with their phones out, talking to each other, yawning, falling asleep, working on their laptops, looking incredibly bored, eating cookies, and even rolling their eyes at your material. You will need to tune out every single one of them because if you allow yourself to get distracted by them, you will freeze up and be completely unable to finish.

You also have to ignore their feedback afterward. I'm not kidding. Because some of it will be positive, and some of it will not. And when it's not positive, trust me, people will not hold back. Cloaked in anonymity, they will criticize what you wore, how you stood, the tone of your voice, your visual aids, the fact that you *had* visual aids, the fact that you *didn't have enough* visual aids, the color of the wall you were standing in front of, the glare on your glasses, your hairstyle, the time of day you spoke, oh and yes, your material (a.k.a. what you actually *said*).

But as you can see, a lot of the feedback is personal. And once this feedback gets posted and lives online, well, then the whole world knows.

Personal sage

Once, after a really important speech at a conference, I sat in front of my laptop reading some tough reviews from the seen-it-all, done-it-all audience. I called Jasmine, one of my personal sages and a very experienced public speaker, to cry. What she told me not only changed my approach to public speaking, it changed my approach to life.

"You've got to get over this," she said. "What are you supposed to do — stand at the exit and ask every single person, 'Did you like me? Good! Oh, and did you? Okay. What about you? No? Why?!' You'll go nuts, and most of all, it would be a waste of time. They're each going to have their own comments, and they'll probably all be different. You may remind some of them of their best friend. You might trigger others about the worst manager they ever had, or someone named Diana who broke their heart last year. You can't control any of that, so don't try. The only thing you can control is the quality of your message."

There's that great saying that's actually a book by Terry Cole-Whittaker, *What You Think of Me Is None of My Business*. I think Jasmine showed me why that's so true. And what was a lesson about public speaking became a much bigger lesson in my life. Walking around looking for everyone's approval for my choices, my lifestyle, my performance, my haircut, whatever, is a beeline to Crazytown.

That's why approval-seeking blocks the yes that changes everything: if so much of our emotional and spiritual and intellectual bandwidth is taken up by looking for and then trying (in vain) to shape our choices and actions to please people, there won't be a millimeter of space for the quality of yes in our lives that brings freshness and beauty and light to us.

So, beautiful someone, let's just control the quality of our message, of our actions, of our happy, healthy, sane lives…and forget about trying to get the approval of everyone within a 5-mile radius of us.

There — done!

We are free.

YES CHANGES EVERYTHING!

We are already brave

"Courage doesn't always roar. Sometimes courage is the quiet voice at the end of the day saying, 'I will try again tomorrow.'"

— Mary Anne Radmacher
Artist

Should. It's got to be one of the most annoying words in any language.

"You *should* just do it," "You *shouldn't* be going out with her," "You *should* be making more money," "You *should* get Invisalign to fix that wonky tooth of yours." Or even self-directed: "I *should* never have left my job," "I *shouldn't* have taken so many credits this semester."

Should usually looks back with regret or forward with unfair demands. These kinds of statements are incredibly unhelpful, and they leave us with this head-scratcher: "Okay, but I [can't/don't want to/am not ready/already did]...so what do I do now?"

In the same way, telling anyone, "You *should* have courage" — doesn't help at all. "Yeah, I know, but I don't, so what am I supposed to do?"

You know what, though? We think of courage as something we have or don't have. "I just don't have the courage" or "I'm just not brave" or "[He/she/they] are just braver than I am." But I don't think courage is something we necessarily *have*. Most times, courage doesn't just bubble up from a well somewhere inside us and move our feet forward or vibrate our vocal cords or poke us in the ribs so we magically raise our hand.

After a courageous choice, we don't look back and say, "I decided I was going to tap into my courage reserves. My tank was 80 percent full, so I had enough to get me through this decision."

On purpose
Courage is much more deliberate and on-purpose, much less spontaneous and natural. (And if it isn't deliberate and on purpose, sometimes even gritty, I think, it's not actually courage!)

So courage isn't something we *have* — it's something we *show* by being willing to take a chance. Sometimes even with our eyes closed. We just, just, just let our feet leave the ledge and trust that our cape will pop open and let us fly.

Courage is *conscious*, a deliberate choice.

> It's saying yes to the job we don't feel 100 percent ready for because we know no matter how afraid we feel, it's the right decision.
>
> It's the decision to speak up about injustice when staying quiet feels safer and definitely less complicated.
>
> It's the choice to raise our shaking hand to volunteer for a tough project when we'd be much more comfortable grabbing a glass of wine with friends.

It's signing the mortgage we know is going to put a crimp in our mad money for a while but is, in every other way, the right long-term investment.

It's walking up to introduce ourselves to someone we want to meet even though we're facing a better than 50/50 chance of rejection.

It's writing books with no guarantee that anyone will want to read them ☺.

When we operate with this quality of courage — the kind we don't wait to feel — we're acknowledging that yes is a chance: things may go well, they may not, or maybe a little bit of both:

Yes to a marriage: a lasting commitment to one person — from blue skies to tornadoes and back again (and again).

Yes to a child: a lifetime and beyond of being completely devoted to another human being down to our bone marrow through every age and stage.

Yes to a mortgage: 15 or 30 years out into the future, when the money flows — and when it doesn't.

Yes to a career choice, especially one that involves a certification or degree: years of money and effort.

Yes to a kitty or puppy: 12+ years and who knows how many chewed chair legs and torn up sweaters and rugs.

Yes to a job change: leaving what's known, whether we love it or not.

Courage is our feet moving forward, our hand dialing the phone, our fingers typing the email, our mouths curving into a shaky smile, our booties firmly planted in a chair outside someone's office when they've ignored every one of our emails and calls ...when we don't feel like doing any of those things, and especially when they scare the bleep out of us!

This means that the yes that changes everything *does* take courage, but we can't wait around to feel it.

Courage doesn't mean we *feel* brave. It means we *act* brave. We do it without waiting for our feelings to catch up and trust that the feelings will follow.

What courage sounds like

Acting with courage is key to the yes the changes everything. By definition, the yes the changes everything is a step into the unknown and the unexplored. Even the yes that lets in more of what we already know is different from yesterday's version of yes.

Here's what courage sounds like in the yes the changes everything:

- "You know what? I've thought it through, I'm scared, but it's right, and I'm going to do it."
- "I'm going to give it a go. There's a good upside to it. Let's see what happens."
- "Wish I'd started earlier, but better late than never."

- "I really believe this will be worth it in the long run."
- "Yes, I'm scared, but for as long as I can remember, I've wanted to get a law degree."
- "Yes, I'm nervous, but I really do want to meet her."

Courage vs. intuition

Courage or not, we should never go against our intuition, that sixth sense that lets us know something without evidence or concrete information. We should never use our yes superpower just because we feel, "Screw it. I'm just going to go ahead with this because I'm sick of being scared/broke/frustrated," or "I'm so tired of thinking about it. I'm just gonna go ahead and do it" — when our gut is telling us it's not a good idea, maybe it's even a really bad one.

You know, every good craftsperson knows the tools of their trade: the right tools to use, when and how to use them. *Master* craftspeople though, are in a league of their own. They know not only what their tools can do, they're also extremely attuned to what those tools *can't* do. Masters know the capabilities of their tools, as well as their limits.

Bear with me because I want to apply this to us. Sometimes, a choice may seem right, all the intellectual facts support going ahead with it...

- He/she says all the right things.
- The job in Chicago has great benefits, good opportunities for advancement, and the company will pay for relocation.

- The apartment we want to buy is close to work, spacious, and available for the right price.

Still, for some reason, we hesitate.

There's the temptation to say, "What is *wrong* with me — this is so perfect! I think I'm just being a wimp about it." But beautiful someone, when we hesitate, there's a reason. Something is going on intuitively that we need to trust and pay attention to.

You know how we tell our kids that if they ever feel uncomfortable in a situation — afraid, queasy, weirded out in any way — they *must* trust that feeling and walk away, or say no, or call us, or all three? Lately with my own kids I've started to shorthand it: "Listen to your gut — it never lies." And it's true that our brains sometimes rationalize, "reason" things out, or make excuses, but our stomachs can't do these things. Which is why when our guts are talking to us, they are telling the truth.

Genius

Our intuition is a form of genius and listening to it means that we respect the limits of the supercomputer in our heads. As the master craftsperson of our own lives, sometimes we need to put the tool (brain) back in the toolbox and just trust our guts.

I've seriously got to put turning off my brain and trusting my gut high on the list of lessons I wish I'd gotten much earlier in my life — maybe you do too? (Let's make this list one day, beautiful someone.) Specifically, to know that when my stomach is twisting, or just giving me that feeling of *yech*, it's talking to me, and this purity of communication, its simplicity, its wordlessness, its inability to make excuses, is often so much smarter than I am in my head. We have both head and heart (intellect and intuition) because we're supposed to *use* both in our decision making.

But we all cut our teeth on objectivity, information, and facts. We've actually been conditioned to be suspicious of intuition — how we vibe in a situation — as something airy and unreal. Frivolous and silly. But thinking this way is tantamount to ignoring one of the most important tools we've been given as human beings.

Our intuition, our Spidey senses, our gut feelings, our deepest memories imprinted on the hippocampus during times of great stress — none of these communicates to us rationally through cognition, through conscious thoughts and words. And yet each is incredibly valuable for making choices that lead to an awesome life — a healthy, whole, and sane one.

Sometimes, we just need to let our gut win.

"The sale ends in 30 minutes!"
While we're on the topic of intuition, please take this to heart, beautiful someone: anyone who is trying to rush us into a quick decision, especially when they see us taking the time we need to decide whether it's right for us, does NOT have our best interests at heart. There's a very good chance they're rushing us because they know that if we have a chance to think about it, we won't do what they want.

That could be as mundane as buying a mattress ("The sale ends in 30 minutes! What's keeping you from buying this right now?"), skiing the black diamond slope for the first time ("Oh come on, you're definitely ready for it!"), tasting alligator meat (what if it's not "just like chicken"?), or (definitely) signing anything on the dotted line!

Let's trust our guts here in a big way: if our stomachs are talking to us, like we're just getting that icky, queasy feeling, let's promise each other we'll walk away and/or buy ourselves some time. We'll let our stomachs win. They will never let us down.

Any decision, especially a big one, made under duress will lead to regrets. Time and again. Without question.

And so we walk.

Quickly.

The other way.

Part 2

DIANA DAVIN

"Only good things"

"When you reach for the stars, you may not quite get one, but you won't come up with a handful of mud either."

— Leo Burnett
Advertising executive

A friend signed a card she sent me during a really rough time in my life using this phrase. "Only good things," she wrote, then signed her name.

It's a sweet memory and such a wonderful wish for anyone from someone who cares about them.

I feel this way about you, beautiful someone. I wish you only good things. And I know that the yes the changes everything can bring them to you.

The yes that changes everything opens the door to our lives and says, "Come on in!" With its good energy and positive purpose, it acknowledges that life is big and delicious and full of adventures waiting for us. It gets us off the sidelines or off the couch and out into new experiences and positive change, helping us build a life that's rich and full of juice and joy, not only for us but for the people we love and care about.

Yes, the *right* yes, opens our hearts and minds and arms to opportunities to experience life to the fullest.

It pushes us out of comfort zones so we learn and grow as humans.

It actively seeks information, experiences, and people who can teach us something good.

And because of all this...

1. Yes builds our confidence
2. Yes is a fountain of youth
3. Yes brings discovery
4. Yes makes us optimistic
5. Yes multiplies happiness
6. Yes feeds our creative spirit
7. Yes is self-love
8. Yes protects us from cynicism
9. Yes shows us how incredibly powerful we really are

...and yes protects our hearts with an insulation of hope. Implicit in yes is a belief that something better is possible, that the future can be different in good ways for us and the people we love.

Yes builds our confidence

"What qualities do you want to build in your life?" So many people answer this question by saying they want to be more confident. Confident in general, confident like him or her, confident about a skill, confident that they're doing the right things with their jobs, loves, lives, and confident in their ability to try new things, handle tough situations, and solve problems.

What builds confidence? Research and information (doing our homework on a new neighborhood we're interested in, getting the details about a new degree program, digging into the background and investments of a company that reached out to us with a potential job, prepping for a job interview by anticipating the questions we're likely to get asked), repetition of a skill we want to build, encouragement from a mentor or friend we trust who tells us we can totally handle a challenge we're facing...all these are confidence-boosting.

But by far the greatest contributor to confidence is *experience*, and in order to get it, we've got to say yes. Experiences of all kinds, including adventures and experiments that *don't* go well, give us the incredible blessing of unforgettable lessons and the best preparation to knock it out of the park next time.

Think about it: if you had to name one thing you're confident you can do, no question, what would it be? Grow tomatoes?

Pick an excellent craft beer?

    Make a blueberry pie?

        Fix a flat tire?

            Change your car oil?

                Make dinner for 20 people?

                    Paint a flower?

                        Run a meeting?

Think of that thing, then answer this question: how do you know you can do it? What gives you that confidence? High on that list: *experience*. Chances are it's something you've done 100 times.

Now think of the first time you did it — the first time you said yes to it. It took determination to suck at it, mess it up, be embarrassed, get frustrated — but then, you persisted, and experience added one brick then another to what became a solid, unshakeable wall of aptitude and confidence.

Through that persistence (i.e., your willingness to say yes to it over and over), your self-image shifted: you began to see yourself as the kind of person who can take on that thing and crush it. That talent, that skill — it's now part of who you are.

This is a mini-miracle, beautiful someone, because repetition strengthens our skill, and that changes how we see ourselves. When we see ourselves as the type of person who takes on a challenge, it builds our self-esteem (a.k.a., confidence, self-understanding, and personal power).

Seeing it through
One of the best feelings is being able to say, "Wow, I did that!" especially when it's followed by, "I never would have believed I could do something like that." How deliciously satisfying and strengthening it is to say yes to a challenge and see it through.

This yes changes everything by sparking an upward spiral; one yes leads to the next, building momentum and lifting us up as we got better and better at this thing, this skill...then higher up, and higher still. And it all began with that first yes. That was the start of this juicy jolt of energy that built our skill and self-esteem at the same time.

The same thing is true when we're on the receiving end: we intuitively know the value of experience in the services we use. As a customer, no matter what service we're buying, it's best (sometimes essential) to have it delivered by someone with *experience*. Not someone with just a degree. Not someone who read a book about oral surgery and is willing to try it out on our root canal (um, that would be *such* a hard pass). Not someone who "really likes flowers" doing the arrangements for our wedding, but someone with experience handling a job of that size so we can be sure everything will go well.

Just doing it
What if we say yes to something and it's *not* a smashing success? What if it's even an epic fail? We all know how

hard it is to stand up and get back in the game after a face plant.

But pan out for the big picture:

Just taking on a challenge matters a lot, regardless of the result. Facing it lets us see ourselves as the type of people who say yes to new experiences, believe a better future is possible, face tough stuff early and often. We say yes to goals, speak out and take action according to our beliefs, push past obstacles, do the right thing no matter how hard it is. And through it all, we learn, grow, and get more powerful and less afraid.

We start to say things like:

- "Been there. No worries…this will be all right!"
- "That was a tough experience, but I landed on my feet."
- "I don't stress about that anymore. I've been through it before, and it's really not that big a deal."
- "The first time that happened was hard, but I'm so much stronger now."

So there is real confidence-building power in just doing it. In seeing ourselves turning toward a challenge and taking it head on.

"That way doesn't work"

And when things aren't a smashing success, we become the type of people who grab the bad experience by the shoulders and shake it, demanding that it teach us something: "Oh, you're not getting out of here that easy! You've got to make this worth something by telling me what happened and what I can do next time so I never have to see you again!"

Maybe the answer is:

- "That way doesn't work."
- "I needed more help than I asked for."
- "I kinda rushed in. I'll go slower next time."
- "Wow, I can't actually die of embarrassment."
- "Guess I'm not great at multitasking, especially big goals. I really need to focus on one thing at a time."
- "So I went to law school, started practicing law. Then I realized I hated law, but really loved wine. Now I'm starting a vineyard with my wife."

"Look at a day when you are supremely satisfied at the end," said Margaret Thatcher, former Prime Minister of England. "It's not a day when you lounge around doing nothing; it's a day you've had everything to do and you've done it," She was definitely talking about the joy of work and the importance of action, but maybe we can read between the lines a little bit: she doesn't say that everything was a tremendous groundbreaking super-success. She says just the effort and the experience itself matters. Just that you did it. Just that I did it.

Having this attitude about experiences that don't go well is part of what builds our confidence, because every time we go through something tough, we come out the other side of the experience, maybe a little dusty and dinged up, but definitely smarter and stronger.

And more beautiful for the wear.

Experiences that challenge us change us

I always feel sorry for lottery winners or people who have inherited wealth — I really do — because without the financial and professional challenges and yes, *struggles* of life, they are so much more prone to depression. They feel weak because their spiritual and intellectual muscles aren't facing the resistance they need to get strong. They're often scared and maybe defensive because their guts aren't being tested, and they don't have confidence in how they'd react if they were. They haven't had the joy of seeing themselves rise to new challenges. It's just impossible to underestimate the incredible importance of meaningful work and life challenges and experiences.

Think of the stories of young performers or movie stars who've made tons of money before they're even 25 years old and therefore "don't have to work a day in their lives": too many of them fall into deep depression and even self-destructive habits. There's a reason for this, and I don't think that we need to have a lot of psychological science or case studies to know what it is. As humans, we crave challenge. It makes us feel alive and strong and capable and confident. Without it, our souls and self-esteem truly suffer.

Facing tough times

We actually, in truth, in our hearts don't want to have everything handed to us. It doesn't make us feel valuable or strong or capable or confident. It can even be crippling. We need to prove to ourselves how strong we are. How powerful we are, how able to run back into the metaphorical flames and phoenix out of them again and again.

This has to be one of the reasons that when we face tough times in our lives, so many of us say the same thing: "At least I got to go to work," and "I feel so much better when I'm at work. It lets me focus on something other than what I'm going through," and "I don't know what I would have done during that tough time without my job/profession/kids/business to focus on."

We need enterprise; we need work. It makes us strong. It gives us resilience.

This is why challenging experiences, growth and confidence all go hand-in-hand. It's why I tell my kids that not every experience that's good for us feels good when it's happening. Not liking camp, being embarrassed when they lose a game, the first day of...*anything*, being corrected by a coach or teacher...all these and more are making them stronger, more resilient, and smarter, in ways that positive experiences just *can't*.

Tough experiences are a life-long gift because we tend to remember them long afterward. Whether that helps us not repeat a mistake, stay away from certain types of people, turn down job offers that aren't right for us, or anything else we learned about "the hard way."

When we embrace this, we can say yes to tough experiences and bumpy roads and tough climbs that we know will activate our minds and muscles. These challenges make us excited to get up in the morning and face the day, with energy flowing through us, electrifying every corner of our bodies. We feel focused and alive, resourceful and creative.

Oh, yes we do.

Confident humility

Sounds like an oxymoron...kind of like, "I'm proud of my humility."

But here's what "confident humility" means: detaching from the outcome of any situation that we delve into. It means getting to the point of thinking, "Okay, I'm doing this, and no matter what happens, I will not have my identity negatively influenced by this one outcome." Because, honestly? No single experience defines us. No single person, or day or event. Beautiful someone, we can always reinvent today, starting now. Remembering this makes it easier to face new challenges, yes-first.

A long time ago, a wisewoman said something that changed my life: "Imagine how powerful you'd be if it was impossible to insult you." (Oooh, yeah, I — wait, what? I am *not* easily insulted!! ☺)

Now on a good day, when we're feeling strong and positive, even the most annoying situations just roll off our backs. Even the rudest comeback, the meanest post, the most thoughtless action coming at us is like, "Oh well, whatever. Their loss." Other days though, not so much. It's like we're a raw nerve that's incredibly easy to insult. (No judgment here. We're human, and I'm at the front of the line!) It happens...it just does.

But back to that wisewoman: it's true that being impossible to offend makes us powerful, even a special kind of invincible. No matter how irritating or upsetting something is, or more on-topic, no matter how badly an experience goes, we're steady. We hear it, but we're nonreactive, unoffended.

This is confident humility. We have such strong confidence that any insult coming at us is somewhere on a continuum between, "Whatever," and "That might be a good point." So, we said yes, but then — *then* — there was an epic fail, a face plant, broken trust, an unreachable goal.

And instead of anger, frustration, and maybe a dash of self-pity, the experience is like, well, like life itself.

Because here's the thing beautiful someone: the anger, frustration, sadness, grief — all of it is one giant energy vampire that can, if we let it, suck the juice out of whatever positive thing we're trying to do for ourselves and the people we love. Humility is jet fuel because it preserves our energy and focus for brand-new fresh yeses in our lives that have the power to move us forward and create the future of our dreams.

As a bonus, humility enables us to relax and not be in fight mode all the time, trying to correct everyone's ideas and perceptions of us and what we're doing.

Whatever, whatever, whatever with a dash of *so-what?*

Having the humility to wipe the egg off our faces (I'm thinking about the workshops and speeches I gave to rooms of mostly empty chairs, the projects I took on that I really wasn't qualified for and this became painfully apparent in front of a pretty big group of executives, the drawing class I went to thinking everyone was a beginner like me until we turned our easels around to display our work and mine was a wiggly cartoon amid a sea of da Vinci's), but knowing they're still *our* faces: under it all, we define who we are and how confident we feel.

When we say yes, the self-confidence we feel may come from the outcome, but more of it comes from opening our arms and welcoming the experience in the first place. Just taking on the challenge, chin lifted, shoulders back, cheeky look on our faces, maybe with an impish, "I can, and I will," a dash of defiance — it's all part of the picture; it's all part of yes changing everything.

Yes changes everything because it's the thrill of the adventure into the new the different and the unexplored that builds our self-confidence — not the outcome.
So let's promise each other that when we take on a challenge and the outcome is not great, we will never say:

- "That was an epic mistake!"
- "I'm never going to try something like that again!"
- "I am so stupid for doing that!"
- "Why do I always choose the wrong guys/food/friends/jobs/movies?"

Let this be our mantra: "Whatever, whatever, whatever" with a dash of "so-what?" So that we can enjoy the incredible power surge that comes from our confident humility.

And we exhale

A jolt of confidence

Saying yes to a new experience jolts our confidence in a positive way. Suddenly, we're confident that we are:

- Creative
- Smart
- Determined
- Curious
- Resourceful
- Outgoing
- Capable

You know what I mean, beautiful someone? These are the kinds of labels we can confidently apply to ourselves once we have tried something new or continued to push toward a goal we really care about even when the going gets tough. Could be getting a JD or MBA or another chunky achievement like buying a first house, starting to foster rescue animals, or opening a business.

But challenges don't have to be huge to enable us to see ourselves as creative, smart, determined, curious, resourceful, outgoing or capable (or all of these!). They can be just walking up to meet someone new, getting to the gym twice a week for three months straight, finally learning Photoshop — or anything else!

Just notice that each of those examples has something in common: each one requires us to say yes. "Yes, I'd like to meet someone." "Yes, I'm going to hit the weight room and build my strength." "Yes, I will organize my gazillion pictures and start to work on enhancing a few of them in Photoshop."

Yes — yes — yes!

DIANA DAVIN

Yes is a fountain of youth

I head into CVS for cotton balls and polish remover — that's it, that's all I'm getting.

That. Is. All.

Except that when I get there, right away my eyes (and my feet) are drawn to the shiny lip glosses, sparkly eyeshadows, foundations that promise smooth clear skin...and every cosmetic do-dad under the sun.

Do I have that color? Have I tried that brand? Would that foundation work on me? Oooo this one's organic — I gotta try that...it's good for me!

I'm not proud of myself for this. And it happens a lot. My bathroom countertop and drawers are home to a rainbow of colors, finishes, and applicators. Organic and not. Glossy and matte. Sticks and pots. Sponges, brushes, swabs, and wands. Most I've tried. Some are actually still sealed. The fewest are the ones I actually *use*.

I seem to be in a never-ending search for the potion or lotion that is going to make me walk out into the world, not with the face I actually have, but with one I can create. One that's brighter, more colorful, smoother, and let's just say it — younger.

I'm learning though that youth isn't really what I'm after. I mean if you asked me do you want to go back and be 25 or 30 again, um no. I don't want to re-live all those awkward situations, job uncertainties, bad relationships, boundary-crashing relatives — all just to get rid of a few smile lines and scattered grays. What I'm searching for is the *feeling* of being young — hopeful with the best of life out ahead of me, positive and invincible.

Ahh...this thing I want so much isn't a *thing* at all!

Okay so no one is really invincible — got that memo somewhere in my early 30s — but the rest? Hope-filled? Positive? Those I can do. And I don't need to spend money, drive anywhere, or clutter up my bathroom. (Or be disappointed, again, at the way anything pink looks on my face. Oh, don't even ask, but yeah.)

I just need to be open to new ideas and people and experiences. I need to allow myself the life-giving exhilaration of a yes that changes everything. That exhilaration does more for the youthfulness of our faces (and the rest of our bodies) than any product we can buy and apply.

Psyche and soma
Science has found strong links between the psyche (our minds) and soma (our bodies). There are complex connections between our bodies' central nervous system (the brain and spinal cord) and autonomic nervous system (everything else). At one point, it was believed that these systems worked independently of each other, but the field of Psychoneuroimmunology or PNI has proven otherwise. These systems are intimately linked.

And beautiful someone, we don't even need to dig into science to know how real this is: we get a great cut and style at the salon and walk out feeling more clearheaded and fresh.

We clean and organize our home office and feel instantly more productive in it.

Go through the car wash, pull out onto the road, and feel like the car actually *drives* better.

The interplay between our physical experiences and surroundings and the health of our mindset and sense of hope and possibility is undeniable. We experience it all the time in everyday life.

And for these reasons, the yes that changes everything is a fountain of youth for us. Every yes that has the power to change everything is a new beginning — and isn't that the very definition of youth?

Maybe the best part — there's no expiration date on that bottle!

Age is a number; old is a way of thinking

I know people (maybe you do too?) in their 40s who may as well check out right now. They are so totally negative, angry, and down. Being around them feels unhealthy, like I just want to get away as fast as possible. They have all the answers, and all the answers are no, or some variation like, "That doesn't work" or "That's no good" or "People are awful" or "No one cares" or "Everything always goes wrong."

Sometimes it feels like they're waiting for any opening — doesn't even matter how benign it is. Like buying flowers or hiring a mover or getting a coffee or flying to

Miami. The words are barely out of our mouths before we hear:

- "Every florist I know always cheats you with week-old flowers. They die the minute you put them in a vase."
- "Oh yeah? Good luck with that. Moving companies break everything!"
- "Their coffee is so bad…it always tastes burnt. I think they must hire the worst people! I mean, how hard is it to make coffee?"
- "You better make sure you have a lot of time for connecting flights! I've missed the last three connections I needed to make and had to sleep at the airport!!"

Then there are people in their 60s, 70s and beyond who are inspiring and full of energy and ideas. When things don't go well, they say things like, "No worries! All's well that ends well!" "Don't sweat the small stuff!" and "Are you kidding? This is *nothing*!"

They're excited about new projects and adventures, and they use their incredible life experience and perspective to calm situations and make life easier by reassuring everyone around them. Their lives are full of yes. Of being open to new ideas and experiences and people.

So two groups:

- The "Been-there-done-that," "I-know-everything," "You're-not-going-to-tell-me-anything," and "Everything-sucks" crowd.

…and

- The "Oh! Cool!" and "Wow, how great is that?" and "I'm taking a course in that," "I just started working with a personal trainer, even though I've never worked out a day in my life!" "That's so interesting!" "I'm learning how to paint with acrylics!" crowd.

If we think about it, the second group is the complete opposite of old, even though they could be in their 80s. They are the yes crowd. The ones who live young, regardless of the year they were born.

Because *age is a number; old is a way of thinking*.

You know what this means, beautiful someone? Wherever we are in our life journey, the habit of yes is one we best start now!

If you've never heard Bob Dylan's song, *My Back Pages*, give it a listen. As we think about the yes that changes everything, listen to his transformational words at the end of this verse:

> Crimson flames tied through my ears, rollin' high and mighty traps
> Pounced with fire on flaming roads using ideas as my maps.
> "We'll meet on edges, soon," said I, proud 'neath heated brow.
> Ah, but I was so much older then; I'm younger than that now.

Create

My friend Cate told me about an acting teacher who used to say, "It's so much easier to destroy than to create." This was in the context of creating a character the students needed to portray by finding that character's traits within themselves. The teacher's point was that it was so much easier for the students to say, "Forget it! I can't do that!" as in: "I could never play an attorney passionately defending a murderer, a starving artist battling crippling depression, a ruthless money-hungry CEO, or a violent angry father!" than it was to look inside themselves and (super-scary) actually find the traits they needed to portray in these difficult characters.

That teacher's point is also helpful for us, beautiful someone, as we work on the yes that changes everything: in life, it is so much easier to say, "No, I can't," "That's no good," "That's not possible," or "That's ridiculous!"— essentially to make all kinds of statements that are destructive to newness and creativity and possibility and hope — than it is to say yes, as in: "Huh, maybe that could work" or "Sounds tough, but it could be a good idea" or "I've never tried that before, but there's always a first time!" or "Maybe they have a point" or "Yes, that's much better than my idea!"

Yes is work and effort; the other is literally the opposite.

And even though a life filled with dismissive no's can be *easier*, it's not *better*.

It is work to listen for a seed of possibility in an idea, to find something good in what we're hearing, extract it, and use it as a kernel of creativity. That's so much harder than blowing it off with a quick, dismissive, "No way!"

As we venture into our happy, healthy, sane lives together, beautiful someone, let's find the emotional strength to dig for that small seed of yes and use it to create amazing things for ourselves and the people we love.

DIANA DAVIN

YES CHANGES EVERYTHING!

Yes brings discovery

The lightbulb, antibiotics, dark matter, water on Mars...every time, discovery began with yes!

- "Yes, it's possible."
- "Yes, we can do it/find it/make it happen."
- "Yes, let's keep trying."
- "Yes, it's worth finding out."
- "Yes, we will be patient."
- "Yes, there are other ways even if the 100 we tried didn't work."
- "Yes, we will ignore the naysayers."
- "Yes, we'll find the money to do it."

There are thousands more examples of yeses that sparked discoveries and changed the course of history. This is because yes invites fresh ideas and new beginnings. It opens our minds and hearts to let in the new, the different, and the unexplored. In fact, discovery isn't possible without it.

And the power of yes for discoveries of world-changing importance is also inherent in the yeses in our lives:

- "Yes, I'd like to get my MBA."
- "Yes, I'm going to find out how I can change my diet to get healthier."
- "Yes, I'll keep going even though I don't feel like it."
- "Yes, I don't know if she's interested, but I'd really like to meet her."
- "Yes, I'm gonna join that recovery group. I've heard good things about it."

- "Yes, I'm open to finding out if *I'm* the one who needs to change."

Waaaay outside

Discovery by definition takes us outside our comfort zones, where we're used to living, loving, and working — sometimes *waaaay* outside.

And as a creature of habit and someone who really hates to be uncomfortable (leggings/T-shirts/clogs? Literally *every day*), I get it. I have to fight the urge to stay nestled in my comfort zones.

But if we don't let yes force us out of those comfort zones, it costs us — a lot:

- We don't challenge the status quo.
- We become unaccustomed to trying new things, even simple ones.
- We don't examine our own opinions for signs of aging.
- We don't learn.
- We never meet anyone new.
- We don't grow.
- We feel afraid of change.
- We don't have (or let in) new ideas.
- We're not curious.

Wow, that's a tough list to look at. Even considering reaching a point in our lives when we feel this way is scary.

Stepping out of comfort zones is necessary to live rather than just exist. To experience life rather than let it happen to us. (And the more we stretch our comfort zones, the bigger they get, expanding the fields of possibility in our lives.)

So now, what if we flip the list? When we invite new ideas and people and experiences into our lives with yes that changes everything...

- We *will* challenge the status quo.
- We'll *always* be ready and willing to try new things.
- We'll *look* at our opinions and know when they need a refresh.
- We'll be *lifelong* learners.
- We'll *meet* new people all the time.
- We'll *grow and expand* our horizons as people.
- We'll *embrace* change (and maybe even agitate for it).
- We'll be filled with *new ideas* and eager to hear other people's.
- We'll be *open-minded* and curious.

Ahhhh! Much better!

Yes *is* discovery — we discover the truth, our potential, our purpose, our joy, what matters to us, a new idea, a new technology for getting something done, who we care about, who cares about us.

And in that discovery as we venture into the unknown, yes is a risk that things won't go in the direction we might like. That makes for a different kind of discovery: yes as a way of finding out what we *don't* want, *don't* like, what *doesn't* work (think Edison's 999 ways not to make a lightbulb), who our true friends *aren't*, who we *can't* count on.

In our happy, healthy, sane lives, nothing — no experience, idea, relationship, experiment — is wasted. We make it all worth something by learning from it and turning those lessons into a better next time.

In the words of Julius Caesar, "Veni. Vidi, Vici!" a Latin phrase meaning, "I came; I saw; I conquered!"

Onward!

Yes makes us optimistic

What do you know about Helen Keller? Probably that she was blind and deaf and lived a long and influential life. Me too. But it was only after coming across one of my favorite Helen Keller quotes that I started to look closer at her life and realize how truly remarkable she was.

Helen Keller was born a healthy baby in 1880 on a farm near Tuscumbia, Alabama. At six months, she began to talk and at 12 months to walk. By age 2, however, an illness — later they would speculate scarlet fever or meningitis — had taken Helen's ability to see and hear. She would live in darkness and silence for the rest of her life.

Helen grew up in a loving home, but her family didn't know how best to take care of her, so they let her run free and be wild.

As she grew, her inability to see or hear must have become very frustrating. And the wild and unusual behavior that was cute and acceptable in a baby and a toddler was totally unmanageable in an older child. By age six, she was prone to screaming, tantrums, and rages. People began to say that institutionalizing her was the only solution. But Helen's parents were determined to do all they could and find options for her.

Eventually, they found the Perkins Institution for the Blind in Boston. It was there, through Alexander Graham Bell (yes, that one, inventor of the telephone), that they were put in touch with the woman who became one of the most dedicated teachers of all time: Annie Sullivan.

Annie worked tirelessly with Helen to enable her to make connections between objects she could feel and letters of the alphabet that Annie would draw into the palm of her hand.

If you've seen the movie *The Miracle Worker*, you'll remember the scene at the water pump where Annie holds a seven-year-old Helen's hand under the spray, yelling, "It has a *name*!" and spells *W-A-T-E-R* into the little girl's hand. This is the moment when, slowly and with great difficulty, Helen says, "wa-wa."

Everything happens then in the space of a few minutes as Helen runs from the pump to the ground to the trees to the porch steps and demands to have them spelled into her hand. "Mrs. Keller! Mrs. Keller!" Annie screams, "She knows! She *knows*!" By the end of that day, in the fashion of hand-spelling, Helen had learned more than 30 words.

"The infinite capacity of hope"

From that moment, Helen Keller's world opened. She attended the Horace Mann School for the Deaf in Boston, then the Wright-Humason School for the Deaf in New York City. She worked for decades to learn how to read Braille as well as how to communicate through touch-lip reading, typing, and finger-spelling. She was a formidable opponent as a chess player. She attended Radcliffe College where she proved to be a brilliant and extremely hard-working student, graduating with honors in 1904 and becoming the first deaf-blind person to earn a Bachelor's degree.

Helen Keller became an author, completing her first book, *The Story of My Life*, in 1905. Others would follow, including *The World I Live In*, *Out of the Dark*, *The Song of the Stone Wall*, *The Open Door*, and *Optimism*. Helen had a heart for activism, voicing her views on social and political issues such as women's suffrage, pacifism, labor rights, and anti-militarism.

She worked tirelessly on behalf of people living with disabilities, traveling around the world and even testifying before Congress about the needs of the blind. In 1920, she helped found the powerful and influential American Civil Liberties Union. She received honorary doctoral degrees from five renowned universities around the world, and in 1963 was awarded the Presidential Medal of Freedom.

I love the story of Helen Keller's life and her amazing breakthroughs and contributions. Even more amazing: late in her life, she lamented in an interview that one of her only regrets was that she had not been able to learn to speak properly — her speech was halting and incoherent because she had heard so little of the spoken word before her illness. If she had learned to speak clearly, she said, she could have helped more people. "How much more good could I have done if I had acquired normal speech?" she said through her teacher. "But out of this sorrowful experience, I understand more fully all human strivings, thwarted ambitions, and the infinite capacity of hope." What a poignant example of transforming incredible hardship into lasting good!

All this is a backdrop for one of my all-time favorite quotes about optimism that sparked such an interest in the story of Helen Keller from none other than Helen herself:

> "No pessimist ever discovered the secret of the stars, or sailed to an uncharted land or opened a new doorway for the human spirit."

Yes!

Imagine the bottomless buckets of hope and optimism needed for this quality of thought from someone dealing with the adversity that Helen Keller faced. We can't think of her life by today's standards (many of which she pioneered) of respect, sensitivity, awareness, inclusion, and supportive legal standards for differently-abled people. There were no audiobooks or sophisticated hearing aids. Even elevators were a novelty. She could take nothing for granted. Everything took work. Nothing was easy. Her world was one of obstacles and exclusion.

But Helen Keller recognized possibility and said yes.

- Yes to learning.
- Yes to travel.
- Yes to trying new things.
- Yes to helping others.
- Yes to a life full of achievement and contribution.
- Yes to making a difference as the voice of those with no voice.
- Yes to blazing new trails.
- Yes to standing up for what she believed.

All of this took optimism, the belief that something better was possible despite all indications to the contrary. And not just sit-on-the-sidelines optimism by the way, not the kind that just smiles and says, "It'll be okay; it'll be okay; it'll be okay," but optimism so deep and so courageous that she continued to take action on it until very end of her life in 1968 at age 87.

The sting of "realism"

You know, beautiful someone, optimists like us are often accused of being unrealistic mouthers of happy talk. The cynics and pessimists in our lives tend to look at us with some combination of sympathy and derision for our "head-in-the-clouds" way of looking at everything.

But let's break this down...
What exactly *is* realism? We may hear things like:

- "Knowing all the things that could go wrong."
- "Knowing that you might fail."
- "Being aware of the mistakes you might make."
- "Not putting your faith in someone or something that could disappoint you."
- "Knowing that if it's never been done before, it's probably not possible."
- "Lowering your expectations so you don't get disappointed."

And unfortunately, they all have a ring of truth to them!

Things *can* go wrong. We might *not* succeed. Someone *may* disappoint us (maybe even more than once). Lowering our expectations in any situation *can* help us avoid being disappointed.

But here's what's important to realize: just like saying no is easier than saying yes, these definitions of realism are easier than the alternative. Avoiding uncertainty and stressful situations, steering clear of challenges, lowering our expectations…all these definitely make life easier, but they don't raise us up to higher ground. They don't give us the thrill of rising to a challenge, of knowing what we're capable of, and realizing our truly amazing potential.

To once again recognize the extraordinary soul of Helen Keller, she once said: "Life is either a daring adventure or nothing."

This approach to "realism" is *not* (though it's trying hard to be!) a better way to live. We can be realistic and unhappy. Realistic and unhealthy. Realistic and depressed. Realistic and lonely. Realistic and bored.

And let's also remember that…

- Things may go *right*.
- We might *succeed*.
- Someone may surprise us (in a *good* way).
- It may be *possible*.
- Raising our expectations *may* help us raise the bar on ourselves!

The energy of optimism

"Optimism" is from the Latin word *optimum*: the best thing, the quality of being full of hope and emphasizing the good parts of a situation — the possibilities, the potential for breakthroughs.

Beautiful someone, this isn't just happy talk. Because seeing positive possibilities doesn't mean that's *all* we see! We can also acknowledge the challenges and the difficulties but still believe we have what it takes to push past them. We can take the practical, proactive steps to keep the challenges from derailing us.

The energy of this kind of optimism is unbeatable, the kind that lets us believe in the best and work like mad to bring it about while we still have our feet on the ground, solid. This quality of optimism is wind in our sails. It literally lifts us up and carries us forward, over obstacles and through tough times. The obstacles are there, we know it, we see them, we deal with them, and still we sail to the finish line victorious.

The best kind of attractive
It doesn't matter that things *can* go wrong. They will.

Or that we might *not* succeed. Sometimes we won't.

Or that some people *may* disappoint us. They will — for sure!

I don't really know whether this kind of thinking is "realism," but it sure sounds a lot like pessimism. And that's something we need to avoid at all costs if we want to live happy, healthy, and sane.

Think for a second about a pessimist you know, someone who dwells on problems, constantly complaining about traffic, car insurance, their boss, your boss, shoe prices, the fine print in apartment contracts — whatever.

And when something goes wrong, probably this person talks about every angry negative detail:

- What happened
- When it happened
- How it happened
- Why it happened
- Who was there
- Who wasn't there (but should have been)
- Who said what
- How all this proves that they shouldn't have tried, everyone is out to get them, you can't trust anyone, and blah, blah, blah!

On and on — and on — they go, an endless list of negative and not and no and *ugh*!

Now, picture this person: do they seem happy? Healthy? Excited about their lives? Bet not.

In his book *The Optimistic Child*, Martin Seligman, former President of the American Psychological Association, wrote about the importance of optimism by saying:

> "I have studied pessimism for the last 20 years, and in more than one thousand studies involving more than half a million children and adults, pessimistic people do worse than optimistic people in three ways. First, they get depressed much more often. Second, they achieve less at school, on the job, and on the playing field than their talents augur. Third, their physical health is worse than optimists."

He concludes by saying that a pessimistic view of the world is clearly "a costly one."

And it's true: optimistic people are often pretty successful. They're definitely happy. They are listened to and sought after. Beautiful someone, when we live our lives with healthy grounded optimism — the kind that's positive and hopeful, but still acknowledges obstacles — we are the best kind of attractive. People want to be around our energy and positive take on things. They know that we've made it a practice to see the good in any situation and to be hopeful about the future.

Even when something doesn't go according to plan, we're the ones asking questions like:

- "Okay wait. What went right? There's always something!"
- "What did we learn? What can we do differently next time?"
- "What would have been the best possible outcome in a situation like this? How can we make that happen next time?"

…all questions that can only have positive, hopeful, action-taking answers.

Pretty optimistic of us, no? ☺

DIANA DAVIN

YES CHANGES EVERYTHING!

Yes multiplies happiness

"I was always too broke to travel," my friend Lauren said. "Then too busy. Then too scared of taking off from work for two weeks. But when my friends finally dragged me to Barcelona, I was totally amazed not just at how great it was but how small my life felt up until then. The trip opened my world. Now I have the bug, and I realize how much I was missing by not saying yes to travel."

Take a second to think about it, beautiful someone: are there experiences or ideas or people that your knee-jerk reaction is to say no to? Forget about who or why, just something that out of habit you always turn down?

For me that would be parties — social gatherings of all sizes. I just get really antsy at these kinds of things, especially if I don't know the people really well. My knee-jerk reaction is, "Well that's gonna be stressful, and I'll probably end up standing around and talking to a lot of people I'll never see again."

It's not that I can't be social. I can. I do it all the time, and I'm really good at talking and making people feel comfortable. It's just that I find it exhausting, and I have 100 books that I want to write and acres of gardens that I want to plant and yards of textiles that I want to design and hundreds of dance classes that I want to take. And every time I say yes to one of these gatherings or any adventure really, I think a lot about all the time I'm "wasting" when I could be doing any one of those other things!

I know that sounds kind of sad and maybe a little selfish, but it's the truth!

Also true...

When I make the effort to say yes to parties or unique experiences, my world usually opens up in some way. I meet somebody cool. I visit a city, state, or even a country that I've never been to and learn about it. Almost always, the food is great, and I learn something.

In South Africa, I had some of the most amazing meals of my life, collected shells I'd never seen anywhere (not even in pictures), tasted wine that could only be called nectar of the gods, breathed in chalky, earthy dust from the swish of an elephant's tail, met the most loving people, and swam with penguins at a beach carved out of ancient rock. I was terrified to go and crazed about sitting on a plane for 17+ hours. But I said yes to it, and I'll always be grateful that I did. Since then, I've developed a fascination for South African art, fallen in love with malva pudding, and spent endless hours drawing those shells!

Mihaly Csikszentmihalyi, one of the co-founders of positive psychology, wrote in 1990: "The best moments in our lives are not the passive, receptive, relaxing times...The best moments usually occur if a person's body or mind is stretched to its limits in a voluntary effort to accomplish something difficult and worthwhile."

It's taken me time, but I've learned this!

What about you, beautiful? Can you think of something you said yes to that opened your world, changed your mind, expanded your horizons, brought someone or something new into your circle? And then opened a flood of happiness that flowed in your direction?

"A mind stretched"

U.S. Chief Justice Oliver Wendell Holmes once said (one of my all-time favorite quotes), "A mind stretched by a new experience can never go back to its old dimensions." The experiences of our lives change us — they do. Every one of them shapes us into who we are becoming and changes our expectations of what's possible, what can happen, and what we can make happen. They bring new people, fresh learning and life-long knowledge into our circle.

The right yes — the yes the changes everything — welcomes new experiences into our lives with positive purpose. It opens the door to great things and changes our expectations forever. Suddenly we know what's out there. We know from experience that good things can happen when we go to the party, the play, the meeting, the restaurant, the movie, the museum, the country.

> When we say yes to meeting someone to network and find out they've got great connections, including one that leads to a job at Google (happened to a friend of mine).
>
> When we say, "I'll give it a try" and discover an amazing art museum that transports us through time and across cultures, tucked away in an area of town we've never gone, like a gorgeous pearl hiding in an unassuming oyster shell.
>
> When we leave a party feeling good about being part of a group of people who'll look out for us,

give us ideas, share their good news and ideas with us, tell us about classes, friends, apps we've never heard of, stuff going on that we'd never known about.

A channel of amazing

When we say no, especially when we do it without thinking, just to keep things simple, we are literally shutting down a channel of amazing people, ideas, opportunities, and experiences that could change our lives for the better in the immediate term, and maybe even redirect it in good ways for the long term.

And that channel of positive people and good experiences flows in both directions — out from us but also back toward us...

> We start to attract people who think like us: friends, partners, and coworkers who look at life with the same sense of possibility and potential that we do, people we want to be around who also want to be around us, people we talk to about good news and great ideas and share connections with in a positive energizing network that just keeps expanding.
>
> They're our go-to people when we want to talk about a new idea or brainstorm a fresh solution. They're having lunch with someone we want to meet. They're presenting at the networking event we signed up for. They're introducing us to great connections, telling us about amazing opportunities, and sharing their best ideas with us. And we're doing the same for them.

Because we insist on seeing the possibilities in yes, we make people feel healthy and hopeful. It's easy to be around us. They want to be with us and talk to us because they know we will find even the smallest grain of positive potential and help them build on it.

...and as our reputation for doing all of the above spreads, we get put on the short list for invitations and opportunities of all kinds.

Juice and joy
No question that the simple act of saying yes invites in life's happiness, its juice and joy.

Just look at kids — they live totally in every moment. In fact, there's probably no better example of the phrase, "being in the moment."

When they're upset, they are flat out, crying and yelling — loudly. Then, literally two seconds later, the tears still drying on their cheeks, they're laughing and enjoying a diversion provided by a nearby caregiver.

Kids will tell you the day they're doing something as simple as getting ice cream or going to the park or, definitely, having their birthday party — whatever they are involved in when they're doing it — "This is the *best day* ever!" Translation: they are totally in the moment, nothing else is on their minds. They're enjoying themselves completely, and they're saying (screaming!) it out loud.

Hearing my kids say, "I love this, Mama!" feeling the unbridled joy, the completeness of it, is one of the greatest loves but also lessons of my life. It is the lens through which they are looking at the moment, the purity of the feeling they are having, and the utter unselfconsciousness they show when they just say it out loud, usually at a very high volume and followed by, "When can we do this again?!?!"

This is yes expressed as ultimate, all-consuming joy. There's not a molecule of the moment they're not embracing and giving every ounce of their consciousness to.

The kid's version of yes is total: it's eating ice cream that ends up all over their faces, as they dip their fingers in it to feel the creaminess and the cold, smelling, tasting, seeing ("I want the pink one!" "I like the green one with the chips in it!") Their yes multiplies the joy exponentially, not just for them but for every grown-up around them.

This unbridled joy takes an ice cream cone and turns it into something much bigger and more delicious: a total body experience of complete absorption and pure delight.

Next time you're around kids, watch and listen for the gratitude that just bubbles up from the inside of them and gets blurted out because they just can't contain it. And then feel, beautiful someone, the child in you that can absolutely do the same — just by being all-in on yes.

We all have this power, through our own mind, hands, and vocal cords to create the best life for ourselves and everyone we love, a life that's rich in new experiences, constantly growing, always fresh, full of interesting people and experiences.

And in this way the yes that changes everything literally multiplies the happy.

Yes and *people*

You know, it was interesting that when I looked for cover art for this book, I searched on the words "yes" and "people." Is it a coincidence that every picture was filled with happy people and big smiles?

Another thing I noticed: I couldn't help smiling as I was looking at the pictures!

If yes is happy, and happy is infectious, then yes is infectious. Yes creates more yes.

Yes has a ripple effect: the more it brings into our lives, the more opportunities and people and ideas we have enriching our days and lives. The more we say yes to, the more we have to say yes to: the bigger our network of connections, the more people invite us to be part of good things, the more friends we have, the more art and movies and music and destinations we know about, the more opportunities we have.

More of everything good just flows toward us.

There's a theme here: more, multiplication, exponential increase!

DIANA DAVIN

YES CHANGES EVERYTHING!

Yes feeds our creative spirit

Cool facts about Leonardo Da Vinci:

- Born 1452 in Tuscany near the town of Vinci
- Created detailed drawings of inventions that would not emerge for centuries, such as bicycles, helicopters, and airplanes
- Painted countless masterpieces including most notably the *Mona Lisa* (started 1503, and it was in his studio when he died in 1519, currently at the Louvre) and *The Last Supper* (1495, painted at the Convent of Santa Maria delle Grazie where it remains today)
- Almost exclusively self-educated
- Understood art as intimately connected to science and nature
- Believed: "Learning is the only thing the mind never exhausts, never fears, and never regrets."

Talking about one of the greatest artists that ever lived seemed like a great way to open a chapter about creativity!

What about you? Are you creative? Most people say, "Um, no." They think only the da Vinci's of the world or musicians, writers, and performing artists are creative. *Those* are the people with the secret special inborn talent that the rest of us don't have!

But you know what? I think we're all creative; we just need to think about creativity differently.

Creativity is just bringing something new to life.

When we're stuck for a word, it's creative to look it up or even to ask people around us: "What's another word for *house?*" and then use *sanctuary, dwelling,* or *habitat* in what we're working on.

When we need a baby gift for a friend who's having her third, we want to give something different, fresh, and unique. So it's creative to scroll through Pinterest or Tumblr for ideas. We find a store that sells hand-crocheted llamas and one-of-a-kind monogrammed hats — done!

In this sense — bringing something new to life — creativity just sounds like a happy, healthy everyday life:

- "Yes, I want to do that, so how can I find out…"
- "Yes, that's it! Plus, what if…"
- "Yes, that sounds good, and maybe we should also…"
- "Yes, and we'll need to find out…"
- "Oh yeahhh! And if we do that, we can test out my other idea…"
- "Yes! I've always wanted to try…"

Obviously, the theme is yes! And next thing we know, we're creatively:

- Solving problems
- Making good things happen
- Bringing great people together who end up liking working or just being together
- Seeing new opportunities

- Generating the energy and finding the resources to push past obstacles and reach a goal

...and then standing back, looking at the results, and thinking, "Oh man, I created that!"

Creative mojo
This is so important, beautiful, because nurturing our creativity is all-in for being happy, healthy, and sane.

All. In.

Researchers have found strong links between creativity and self-esteem.

Creativity and healing after trauma.

Creativity and learning.

Creativity and giving voice to feelings people didn't even know they had.

Creativity and problem-solving.

Creativity. Bringing something new to life. Venturing into a skill, a form of expression, a task, an endeavor — anything that lies in a direction we have not yet gone in our happy, healthy, sane lives.

Creativity starts with yes!
It could be yes to oil paints on a fresh canvas, yes to a class in Moroccan cuisine, yes to an online fiction writing course, a pottery workshop, a garden design

seminar, a woodworking workshop…yes to anything that gets our personal, unique creative juices flowing.

Beyond what we might consider "traditional" creativity, it could be yes to an assignment that stretches us in new ways, meeting new people, a change in job or career, a different vacation spot, volunteer work, a new place to live.

Where is your unique creative mojo? What do you need to start saying yes to in order to kindle that creative spark in you?

…and I have to say it: when we go all-in on yes to creativity, we'll have to push past the people who will say things like, "What exactly are you making?" (my answer BTW, is always the same: "This." ☺), "You're *still* working on that? I thought you'd be done weeks ago," "Why are you trying that? You don't know how," "What are you going to do with it when you're done?" "That reminds me of what we did at summer camp crafts."

These are all comments and questions that shut down creativity, making it feel like a silly waste of time. That's literally the opposite of what I'm talking about. This is about soul-nourishing, not impressing anyone or trying to gain approval or even sometimes understanding.

Yes is self-love

Yes is better than perfect. Truly. Because what exactly is "perfection"?

Perfection means meeting a standard, usually one set by someone else, who we may or may not know, who may or may not be an expert, who may or may not have ever done the thing we're considering saying yes to.

Perfection is something we read, heard, or saw under the unspoken headline, "You'll never be this, so why bother trying?"

So we end up wondering what would make us...

- Look perfect?
- Perform perfectly?
- Say the perfect things?
- Find the perfect job?
- Date the perfect person?
- Have the perfect home?
- Be the perfect parent?
- Have the perfect kids?

When perfection is what we're reaching for, we say things like, "I could never speak in front of a group," "I can't write," "I'm not artistic at all," "I do not sing," "I can't dance," or "I have no sense of design."

But we can open our mouths and make sounds. We can pick up a pencil and write words or draw lines and shapes on a piece of paper. We can enjoy a song and move to it. We can pick a gorgeous paint color we love for the kitchen.

We can do all these things — *our* way.

So what we're really saying is, "My way of doing these things doesn't meet some outside and changing standard of what it means to be 'good' at them. Some arbitrary idea shared by people I don't even know and will probably never meet. The way I do these things isn't good enough."

Beautiful someone, pause right here and think about what this does to our happy, healthy, sane lives. The obstacle-erecting, rut-digging shovel this idea takes to our beautiful dreams. These are our dreams — no one else's. Our souls are begging us to stop this and let them look around, take a deep breath, and say, "Of course I'm good enough! Of course, I deserve whatever I'm willing to work for! And so yes, yes, yes!"

Smarter and stronger

The yes that changes everything isn't perfect. But it gives us something better than perfection: *progress*. Every experience that yes brings into our lives makes us smarter and stronger. No matter how well things go (or don't go), yes propels life forward.

Yes is like the messy bun of life: it gets our out of the way in a way that's not perfect, but practical and in its own way, beautiful.

I blogged about this recently in my post, "Beautiful is better than perfect." It's from my book, *You Know What I ~~Should Have~~ Said?*.

YES CHANGES EVERYTHING!

A long time ago, I think I must have been 9 years old, I overheard someone describing a piece of music. "It's not beautiful," she said in a tone that made it clear this was not a compliment. "It's perfect, but it has no heart. So perfect, yes, just not beautiful."

For some reason, this stuck with me, and I think about it all these years later. That a piece of music (or anything or anyone) can seem perfect, but lack something that makes it fall short of beautiful. That there are important differences between perfection and true beauty that make striving for perfection not worth it.

Beauty is layered in meaning and intriguing, the way someone's crooked smile or weird ideas make them attractive and interesting. Or the way we can't stop staring at an abstract painting in vivid but mismatched colors and misaligned textures. Beauty is boundless confidence in a person whose physical attributes would never get them a magazine cover. It's the sexy, fashion-forward outfit rocked by someone you'd expect to see in sweats and flats. Or ocean-deep humility in someone so insanely talented that they could rightly brag about their accomplishments for days but would never dream of it.

For all these reasons, real beauty is in the unexpected, and less (even far less) than perfect can be incredibly beautiful.

This means the less perfect we are, the more mistakes we make, the more beautiful we become. The more interesting, the more complex. It means that we are more beautiful with time and experience. We gather strength, grow in character, and earn wisdom through every mistake, every should have said.

We have to remember this in tough situations that don't go well. The less perfect we are, the better we're getting: smarter, stronger, and more beautiful through every experience.

Samuel Smiles, a Scottish author of — of all things, self-help books during the Victorian era — even then put it succinctly, "We learn wisdom from failure…and probably he who never made a mistake never made a discovery."

It's no coincidence that many great inventions have come about by virtue of a "mistake." Did you know that sticky notes were literally a mistake? A scientist was attempting to formulate a new permanent adhesive, and in his quest ended up creating just the opposite: a bad batch of glue. This glue is what is now on the back of every sticky note. To think that such a "mistake" has become a universal item that we probably couldn't survive without!
One person's bad batch of glue is another's zillion dollar discovery!

There are lots of examples of mistakes that led to discoveries, including chocolate chip cookies and — no kidding — penicillin.

Even when we've made room for yes, decided that the choice in front of us lines up with what we value and has a positive purpose for our lives, there are no guarantees that everything will go as we hoped. There's no perfect moment to act. That moment, the one when we know for absolute sure that if we say yes, everything will turn out just right, no hiccups, no stumbles, no egg on our faces...well, that would be nice, and it does happen every once in a while, but not often.

The perfection cure

And so the yes that changes everything is a great cure for perfectionism. You know what I mean — the kind of thinking that costs us so much. My friend Ian told me, "I wish I had a dollar for every time I hesitated, waiting for the exact right moment to say yes to something — the moment when I knew it was the perfect choice and everything was guaranteed to go right," he said, adding with a wry smile, "I'd be really rich."

I get it — I do. I can get so analytical about what I'm doing that I literally get stuck in place. I learn from past experiences (a good thing), but instead of using those lessons to move forward in a positive way, (now, the not-so-good thing), I use them to go back and try to fix everything that's already done and get hung up on this particular brand of perfectionism that is maybe one step forward and eight steps back. There are about 100 changes that I would make in every book that I've written, but I'm working really hard, beautiful someone, to always move forward and not obsess about making changes to things that have already happened.

And in doing so, I am always mindful of poet Maya Angelou's great consolation: "I did what I knew. Now that I know better, I do better" — one of the most liberating, kind, brimming with self-care quotations ever. It's an honest promise to use whatever happens after yes — good or bad — and not waste it. "Yes, I'm in, and I will make it worth something. It will go well, or I will learn from it, but either way, I'm going to make it valuable." Good information that we can use in the future to shape our awesome lives.

And we're not machines, beautiful someone! It may take a period of mourning to heal after things don't go well — but the final molecules of courage are our absolute commitment to moving forward.

Because here's the thing: while we sit waiting for the perfect moment to say yes, the opportunity in front of us will keep moving. The job will go to someone else. The moment to start the relationship will pass. Someone else will come up with an idea similar to ours and actually move it forward.

Perfection is paralyzing
...it keeps our lives in a holding pattern, waiting for guarantees that just aren't real. In the moment, we hesitate, but perfection's long-term costs are even more dire: it damages our confidence, self-love and self-acceptance. These costs are far more lasting than the momentary loss of an opportunity. And beautiful someone, in our hearts, we know this. We know perfection isn't a thing. Our best effort, good information, help from people we trust, maybe a prayer, and we're off, after it, and, this is key: good with whatever happens next.

Here's our mantra: "I'm willing to try, and if things don't go well, I've got the communication skill, confidence, and maturity to look at the blip (or gigantic mess) and say, 'Okay, so that happened. I'll get back at it, but first I'm going breathe, reflect, and learn...maybe even take a nap.'"

So what?

At its best, self-acceptance is a lifelong process. We're doing it all the time, through every experience and growth spurt. And the yes that changes everything can help us every step of the way.

And yes is a process: things may go great, they may not, or anything in between. Regardless, we learn and move on.

But especially when things don't work out, here's one of the most powerful questions we can ask ourselves: *so what?*

So what if it didn't work out?

So what if she ended up being a jerk?

So what if I decided I should have majored in environmental science instead of engineering?

Ninety-nine percent of our so-whats turn out to be minor in the long run: they weren't one-way streets, weren't permanent, and weren't unfixable.

And so — *so what?*

We have to resist the urge to stay stuck in comfort zones out of perfectionism, living a life unfulfilled, un-realized, un-savored, un-enjoyed. I'm not advocating crazy risk-taking or adrenaline-junkie stuff, just that we try, we put ourselves out there, we don't sit on the sidelines because our first tries are going to be bumpy or messy or, ahem, *imperfect.*

Plus, repeat after me: "I don't need to be perfect to be valuable. I don't need to be perfect to try this, in fact if I'm trying it for the first time, I will not be perfect. I may not even be 'good.' I don't need to be perfect to be legit at anything. I don't need the outside validation that comes from other people, any website, blog, or picture, or any standard that I have arbitrarily created from the outside. I get my cues from the *inside*. I listen to *my own voice...*"

"...and it's telling me to love myself because I am already perfect."

YES CHANGES EVERYTHING!

Yes protects us from cynicism

An easy day hike in the mountains — that's what it should have been — but somehow we got lost. The trail back to the car (or what we thought was the trail) kept looping us back up the mountain instead of down to the trailhead. Tree after tree, rock after rock, we walked...and walked. Afternoon turned into evening, and dark clouds rolled in.

It started to drizzle then outright rain, and still, we were lost, only now we were lost and wet. And muddy. And pissed. We tried one last time to find the way back to the car. Again, we looped up instead of down and came back to the same spot.

This was *not* good.

We had nothing with us: no gear and, except for one pulverized granola bar, no food or water left. It was unavoidable: time to look for a spot on the ground to spend the night. As we snapped at each other over if it was better to sleep under pines or maples and what jacket to use as a pillow, we heard a dog barking, then voices.

Another group of hikers was headed down.

We picked up our stuff, walked with them for half an hour, then finally got our bearings and saw the way out. We took to the trail ahead of them in a sprint. It was full dark by the time we got back to the car. We threw our packs in the trunk, got in, and said not one thing to each other on the way home.

Much later, when we finally did talk about that hike, we remembered feeling incredibly frustrated, but also really exposed and vulnerable.

Since then, whenever I write about cynicism, I think about that day in the mountains and the stress of being exposed, unprotected from the elements. I think this is because it was dangerous to be unprepared in the mountains, but it's also really scary to me to be unprepared for assaults on my plans and dreams — just another way of saying the cynicism that robs us of our hope and sense of possibility. And that's the connection, at least that's the connection my mind always makes.

Cynicism is everywhere!

The headlines that make us feel like everyone is on the take. The bill collectors who call and mail and call and text and email and call and call and *CALL*. Companies who don't seem to care about us as people. Coworkers who don't pull their weight. Friends who aren't loyal. Partners who break promises. Managers who don't have our backs or even try to compete with us for glory.

No matter how strong we are, these experiences can stretch us to the breaking point, until one day, we just snap. The mean people on the phone ("I thought you said this was customer *service*? Seriously?"), friends who aren't there for us when we need them the most, the person who won't let us in on the highway even though it won't cost them a thing, the manager who lets us take the fall for something he did...it all takes a huge toll, and we get so discouraged that we say things like, "People are *awful*," "Why bother trying? Relationships *never* work out," or "Doesn't matter how hard you work. It's all about politics."

This won't be us! Because right now, we gear up. Our equipment: the yes that changes everything, a positive act of defiance that protects us from falling into cynicism. It's the, "Okay, so that happened, but I'm still going to say yes to this."

- "I'm still going to try."
- "Still going to believe in myself and trust my choices."
- "Still going to believe in heroes."
- "Still going to have faith people."
- "Still going to take on extra projects at work."

"Yes. I. Am."

So, beautiful someone, let the world throw fire at us.

We'll phoenix out of it and still say, *yes!*

DIANA DAVIN

YES CHANGES EVERYTHING!

Yes shows us how incredibly powerful we really are

For decades, running the mile in less than four minutes was considered impossible, beyond the physical capacity of the human body. Then one day in 1954 on the Iffley Road track in Oxford, England in front of 3,000 spectators, something incredible happened: a 25-year-old medical student named Roger Bannister ran the mile in 3 minutes and 59.4 seconds.

More amazing than the achievement itself was what happened afterward. Though forever, runners had tried without success to break the four-minute mile, within a few weeks, the record was broken again. In a few years, the mile had been run in less than four minutes hundreds of times. Today, the record stands at just over 3 minutes and 43 seconds.

Years later, Roger Bannister remembered almost changing his mind about the run that day as the winds were strong and unpredictable. Finally though, about 20 minutes before the start, he said yes, and made history. Everyone else shook their heads, but he nodded at an inconceivable goal and rose to an impossible occasion.

In doing so, he changed the impossible to the possible. And not just by baking a better cake. He'd unbounded the physical limits of the human body. He'd ushered in the beginning of a new era in sports. Today's athletes don't see records as limits. They see them as challenges. This is clear as we watch world-class athletes perform:

as each year passes they just take our breath away, whether it's Simone Biles in gymnastics or Michael Phelps in swimming, what they are able to achieve would've been unimaginable a generation ago. Roger Bannister set this mentality in motion by saying yes to a race on a windy day more than 50 years ago.

What must it have been like to learn he had achieved this feat?

I think we know. Yeah, we do. Think about a challenge you rose to, something you tried that you never had before. That time you raised a sweaty hand. Said okay in a shaky voice. Logged in and registered for something with butterflies banging around in your stomach. Signed up for that course in a subject you knew nothing about. Said, "I'm going to try," when everyone else said, "Why bother? It's impossible," or "You? You've never done that!"

We've all risked yes in the past, otherwise we'd all still be where we were ten years ago. We reached further than what we could see from our own window (or job or friend group or relationship or experience or routines), even when we knew it was a stretch, and we surprised ourselves, not always in huge dramatic ways, but we did surprise ourselves.

Challenge, change, and learning

Challenge, change, and learning all go together (usually in that order) for a reason. So we rose to an occasion and found out something. We learned what works, what doesn't, who we can count on, who we can't. What we're capable of, what was too much of a stretch at the time...in other words, something worthwhile, no matter what the actual outcome was.

And the good didn't end there, because what Roger Bannister did broke through not a *physical* barrier as much a *mental* one. His achievement, and more to the point what it set in motion, says a lot about mental barriers that become physical ones in our minds, which can become as solid as a brick wall blocking our way forward. It also speaks to just how powerful we are, what we can accomplish in ways that can absolutely amaze everyone, including ourselves.

And it starts with yes:

- "Yes, I'll try."
- "Yes, I can."
- "Yes, there's hope."
- "Yes, it's possible."
- "Yes, I'd like to see."

"My Next Adventure"

The Becoming Journal includes a section I called "My Next Adventure" that begins with this:

> ***I will dare to be extraordinary.***

> How long has it been since you felt the thrill of reaching for a stretch goal or the tingle of nerves at trying something new?

> Too long?

> Shake things up: stretch into a big challenge. In the bargain, you'll get used to the unpredictable, meet

new people, adapt to new situations, and think of possibilities ("What can I do with this brand new thing?").

The extraordinary starts with yes. We feel so alive when we break out of our regular routine and try something — anything — new.

Literally, anything:

- Studying the Mona Lisa
- Listening to an album by a new artist creating in a musical genre we've never heard before
- Seeing a production by a local theatre company and being blown away by the talent in our own backyard
- Visiting the Planetarium
- Watching a TED Talk on living vegan and the next agricultural revolution

There's a one-of-a-kind energy that just rushes through our systems. I've come to appreciate this more as my life has gotten more complicated and scheduled. There's so much that we have to do every day, every week, every month and every year that it sometimes feels like there isn't room for something new, but that's precisely when freshness becomes essential, even critical to our happy/healthy/sane. Routine can become numbing as we do the same things day in and day out. We begin to feel like machines — less alive, less vital, less human.

So in the midst of our have-to-do's: eat, sleep, brush our teeth, get dressed, make sure kids do all of the same, pay bills, buy bananas, make dinner... the should-do's:

- Work out more often
- Eat better
- Read more
- Watch less
- Call the people we care about
- Enforce date night
- Host at least one holiday a year
- Pray/meditate

...let's say *yes* to our want-to-do's, the adventures:

- Learn to ski
- Try the Whole 30 diet
- Paint the hallway a super-cool color
- Change jobs
- Go back to school
- Move to the city/country
- Stand up and speak out for something we believe in

That's all for now!

> Out beyond ideas of wrongdoing
> and right doing there is a field.
> I will meet you there.
>
> — Rumi
> Sufi poet

We've come to the end of another book together, beautiful someone, and I have to say: I loved writing *Yes Changes Everything!* What began as a sequel to *The Gift of No* became a joy-filled journey of discovery about the power of yes and its ability to create hope, optimism, and a positive future for us.

The yes that changes everything gives life juice and joy, no matter how large or small it may seem. This could be finally saying yes to making our lives a priority with better self-care.

> It could be yes to taking on a new assignment at work with a brand new attitude.
>
> Could be adding a new positive habit, like walking every day or eating more veggies.
>
> Could be reaching out to someone we haven't talked to in a long time, but should.
>
> Or cleaning out a room at home to set up our own studio for painting, pottery, drawing, woodwork-

ing, or anything else that gets our creative juices flowing.

Or raising a hand to volunteer to help.

Or raising our voices about something that matters.

Of course, the yes the changes everything is also opening the door to the big stuff — the new relationship, the new career, the new house.

Doesn't matter.

Our lives and passions are all different, so the yes that changes everything is uniquely life-affirming for each of us — one reason it's off-the-charts important for the happy, healthy, sane lives we're building.

Still, one thing is the same for all of us: yes changes everything because growth lies in any direction we haven't gone yet. Yes moves us away from where inertia is taking us and toward the intentional best that life has for us.

Let's meet there, beautiful someone.

I wish you blue skies,

Diana

www.ingramcontent.com/pod-product-compliance
Lightning Source LLC
LaVergne TN
LVHW011422080426
835512LV00005B/206